MEET
LAURAINE WHITE

A prolific writer, speaker, business professional, and woman of God, Lauraine White has been vice president of several banks, and owned mortgage and real estate companies but left it all behind to follow the call of Christ. She has come to a point in her life where all of her accomplishments mean nothing. Her saying is, "I am so hidden in Christ, that you must first seek Jesus in order to find me." She became lost in writing these books because of the status of the Church and the world today. What she delivers through her writings are timely lessons for every believer in Jesus so that they are equipped to fight life's battles. She is a mother of three adult children, loves to sing and give advice on real estate.

Hello!

Right after 9/11, my world was rocked and hurled to a place I never imagined. I ended up at the intersection of "Heartbreak Lane" and "Defeat Street." It was at that very place that an angel visited me at work (of all places) that took me on a journey of discovering who God really is. That journey of approximately twenty-one years brought me to understand that I have an obligation to teach what I've learned. Maya Angelou once said, "There is no greater agony than bearing an untold story inside you." So, I'm here to challenge your understanding of who God is, who Jesus is, and who you are because of what they did for you. I'm taking this journey with you as I write. It's as if God's thumbprint is sealing every word I write with you in mind. Don't take this moment lightly and don't take it for granted. It's your time.

"Prepare to be challenged."

4

THE WAY OUT MASTER CLASS

GET OUT & STAY OUT

LAURAINE E. WHITE

MIRACLE MOVEMENT

MISSION STATEMENT

We exist to educate, motivate, and inspire those seeking to know God in a deeper way. We help these seekers to build a relationship with Jesus that goes beyond church attendance, singing in a choir or serving on a church board. Furthermore, we establish with seekers of divine knowledge understanding of their identity in Christ, who their enemy is, and how to endure the battles of life. This is accomplished by orchestrating tried and true life strategies that involve prayer, fasting, and the greater works being firmly rooted in them. We believe that miracles, signs and wonders follow us because Jesus's spirit lives in us; therefore, the greater works are done through us.

MIRACLE-MOVEMENT.COM

TABLE OF CONTENTS

Welcome!

I am here to help you see Jesus in a whole new way and to teach foundational principals that will equip you to not only have eternal life in the life to come, but that the life you live here on earth is full of power.

THE CHALLENGE

Prepare to be challenged in ways that you thought were not spiritual, but Jesus wants you to be whole and balanced. If you only consider one aspect of life, you will become lopsided and it will cause you to topple over when life's struggles hit you.

The practical exercises and bible studies that are included in this workbook are what the Holy Spirit used to help me get out of difficult and horrific circumstances that life threw at me. I attribute these events that happened in my life to Satan and the forces of darkness that attacked every area of my life in order for me to give up on God. What didn't kill me, made me stronger. God, through His Holy Spirit used every obstacle that I faced to teach me the art of spiritual warfare. Jesus did the heavy lifting by defeating Satan and giving us the keys to the kingdom of heaven. All we need to do is rest in Him and use what we've been given.

Lauraine White

WHY ARE YOU HERE?

We all have our reasons for coming to a place where we need help. There's no judgment here. This is a safe place for you to become equipped for the battles of life. And your why is essential for us to understand how to proceed in the most effective way to see you obtain the freedom you're seeking.

Jesus came for that reason. He knew you would come to this place seeking help and my life's circumstances caused me to experience intense attacks so that I became equipped to overcome.

You're in the right place at the right time. We overcome by our testimony and my testimony is that God made me a weapon of mass destruction through the things that I dealt with in my own family.

Demons moved into my house and paraded around like pompous kings because they knew I would fear them. What they didn't know is that every encounter that I had with them pushed me to exercise the authority and gifts given to me to overcome. After a time of fasting for 40 days, I watched as demons left my then husband and I've never been the same since.

If you open yourself up to learn this material and become equipped to fight the battles in front of you, you, too, will become a force for Satan to reckon with.

Begin to think about where you know in your heart you want to be a year from now, spiritually. What does that look like? Why is this important to you? **Is Jesus the Lord of your life?** Why or why not?

A QUICK NOTE

"The one who does what is sinful is of the devil, because the devil has been sinning from the beginning. The reason the Son of God appeared was to destroy the devil's work." 1 John 3:8

WHAT'S YOUR WHY?
It's Important For You To Acknowledge

Your "why" is what drives you to do what you do. For some people, it may be that you, too, are dealing with spiritual battles beyond your control. List them out so that you are aware of what motivates you.

My why was I wanted peace in my home and for my loved ones to be free. Little did I know, it would lead me to know God in ways I never dreamed of.

YOUR WHY	WHY NOW?

DISCUSSION TOPIC:

What brought you to this place in time?
Explain in detail.

PART ONE

Identity Crisis

IDENTITY CRISIS

We find that not only is there identity crisis for individuals, but organizations and nations are dealing with identity crises. In fact, churches are in crisis over identity--who do we belong to and knowing who we are.

There needs to be a clear understanding of who we are so that when we associate with organizations, whether it be in business, socially or at our places of worship, we are fully grounded in our identity and not shaken off of our foundation. For some of us, this seems logical but for the rest of us, it requires some work. Even when it appears logical, there are instances that occur that cause us to reevaluate who we are.

Or maybe you're at a crossroad, where you've made the decision that what you were taught no longer aligns with what you have learned to be true. You know that where you are is not where you belong.

You've come to the right course. We will provide you with a platform for you to work through and think through the how's, the why's, and the what's to establish your plan of action. This is a tool to help you do the work necessary to bring about the changes you want to see happen.

As we peel back the layers together, may you find peace in the process and know that you are exactly where God knew you would be. You were created for such a time as this.

Identity Crisis: Why does it exit?

A crisis is defined as "a condition of disorientation and role confusion occurring especially in adolescents as a result of conflicting internal and external experiences, pressures, and expectations and often producing acute anxiety." (The American Heritage® Dictionary of the English Language, 5th Edition) It can also be an emotional event or traumatic change in a person's life brought on by stressful circumstances. This crisis draws us to question the very fabric of our belief system. The questions surrounding identity cannot be answered by the created thing. The true identity of it can only be answered by consulting with its creator.

Identity

A part of our identity is found in who we belong to--who's your daddy? That's not just about who planted sperm in your mother. It's more about who your Father is. Who do you serve? The answer is not found in whether or not you attend church services, sing in a choir or teach a bible study.

The relationship that we're speaking of lies in the crevices of your heart. Is your allegiance to God the Father or Satan? Yes. This is a real question that you need to ask of yourself. What you say doesn't always speak to your actions. So, who's your daddy?

If you believe in God, that's a great answer. Beyond that, do you believe that there is a heaven and a hell? Do you believe in the afterlife? Will there be a final judgment that we all must face, where we will be sentenced to a life of torment or a blissful one in paradise?

These questions are vital in setting the foundation of where we're going in this course, but also it's the groundwork for the life of the believer in Jesus Christ. Recent research, done by the Pew Research Center, shows that one in six adults in the US do not believe in the afterlife.

More Americans believe in heaven than in hell

More Americans believe in heaven than in hell

% of U.S. adults who say they believe in ...

	Heaven %	Hell %
All U.S. adults	73	62
Christian	92	79
Protestant	93	84
Evangelical	96	91
Mainline	88	69
Historically Black	93	89
Catholic	90	74
White Catholic	88	70
Hispanic Catholic	92	79
Unaffiliated	37	28
Atheist	3	1
Agnostic	26	14
Nothing in particular	50	39
Men	68	59
Women	78	65
Ages 18-29	63	55
30-49	69	59
50-64	81	70
65+	79	62
Republican/lean Rep.	85	75
Democrat/lean Dem.	64	52
White, non-Hispanic	72	58
Black, non-Hispanic	88	80
Hispanic	78	66
Northeast	68	51
Midwest	79	67
South	77	69
West	65	54

Note: White and Black adults include those who report being only one race and are not Hispanic. Hispanics are of any race. Source: Survey conducted Sept. 20-26, 2021, among U.S. adults. "Few Americans Blame God or Say Faith Has Been Shaken Amid Pandemic, Other Tragedies".

PEW RESEARCH CENTER

One-in-six Americans do not believe in any afterlife

% of U.S. adults who ...

	%
Believe in both heaven and hell	61
Believe only in heaven	13
Believe only in hell	1
Believe in neither heaven nor hell	26
Believe in an afterlife	7
Do not believe in any afterlife	17
No answer	1

Source: Survey conducted Sept. 20-26, 2021, among U.S. adults.
"Few Americans Blame God or Say Faith Has Been Shaken Amid
Pandemic, Other Tragedies"

PEW RESEARCH CENTER

Among those who believe in an afterlife other than heaven or hell, what do they believe?

Among those who believe in an afterlife other than heaven or hell, what do they believe?

Among the 7% of U.S. adults who say they do not believe in heaven or hell but do believe in some kind of afterlife, % who describe the afterlife as ...

	%
NET Spirit/energy lives on	**21**
Spirit/energy continues to live on	14
Consciousness continues	2
Another dimension/reality	6
NET Reincarnation/coming back	**17**
Reincarnation/enlightenment	9
Cyclical existence/rebirth	8
NET Rejoin universe/universal energy	**8**
Spirit/energy is changed/transformed	4
Rejoin universe/God	6
Learning/growth	**4**
NET Peaceful/happy/without suffering	**11**
Reunited with loved ones	2
Peaceful/happy/without suffering	10
Other/unclear	**9**
No response	**42**

Note: Subcategories do not sum to NET totals shown because respondents could give multiple responses.
Source: Survey conducted Sept. 20-26, 2021, among U.S. adults.
"Few Americans Blame God or Say Faith Has Been Shaken Amid Pandemic, Other Tragedies"

PEW RESEARCH CENTER

"But the [Holy] Spirit explicitly and unmistakably declares that in later times some will turn away from the faith, paying attention instead to deceitful and seductive spirits and doctrines of demons." 1 Timothy 4:1

Identity Crisis

"Study and do your best to present yourself to God approved, a workman [tested by trial] who has no reason to be ashamed, accurately handling and skillfully teaching the word of truth." 2 Timothy 2:15

Read chapters 1 and 2 in "The Way Out" companion book.

In all your getting, get an understanding. Why are we here on earth at this time in history? What is our purpose for living, if this is all there is to life? Where did this notion of no afterlife originate? And who benefits from this type of understanding?

If there is a heaven, what will happen to those that don't believe in it? Are they a shew in, despite their disbelief? Or would they be hell bound without hope of overcoming it?

In juxtaposition to this argument, we can observe our own system of justice, where there is a perception of "law and order." Those that abide by the laws of the land are "free" to go about their daily activities without the fear of being arrested. But when a crime is committed and someone is charged in those crimes, they must stand before a judge or jury of their peers and a judgment is rendered. If they are found guilty, they are punished based on the crime committed and the laws of that jurisdiction.

Just as the world has laws, the Creator of the world has laws. Whether we believe in them or not, they exist. It's important for us to get to know the Creator's laws set for the universe so that we can live a free life here and live in paradise in the life hereafter.

We all know that laws of our land exist, it's our duty to know the laws, not skirt around them. It's in knowing the laws that you find freedom. And it's the same with the laws set by our Creator, God.

This counter message that God isn't real, that heaven and hell are not real, comes from our adversary, the devil. He wants to keep us in the dark about the Truth. This course will teach you the Truth.

DISCUSSION QUESTIONS
Think through the questions before answering

1) Discussion Question: Is God Important to you? Why or why not?

2) Explain briefly your conversion experience? Were you a child, teenager or adult? Was you life really changed?

3) Discussion Question: If you died today, do you know whether or not you're going to heaven? Why or why not?

4) Discussion Question: Are you satisfied with your Christian walk? If not, how would you like to see it improve?

5) Discussion Question: Do you contribute to the quality of your relationships? How?

6) Discussion Question: With regard to family, how do you add value to them?

7) Discussion Question: Are you defined by the work that you do? Please give detail.

8) Discussion Question: With regard to family, how do you add value to them?

9) Discussion Question: Are you defined by the work that you do? Please give detail.

10) Discussion Question: With regard to your emotions or emotional state, what roles do they play in where you are today?

WHAT'S
important?

Rank the top 10 most important things in your life and estimate how much time you spend on them weekly.

IMPORTANT THINGS IN YOUR LIFE

01

02

03

04

05

06

07

08

09

10

REFLECTION NOTES

_____

_____

LIMITING
beliefs

Try to identify other beliefs that are holding you back and how you can reframe them to be more productive.

CURRENT BELIEF	BETTER ALTERNATIVES
CURRENT BELIEF	BETTER ALTERNATIVES
CURRENT BELIEF	BETTER ALTERNATIVES

REFLECTIONS

Use this space to write down what you are hearing from the Holy Spirit as we complete this section. Everything you're experiencing is important to the process of transformation.

R
E
F
L
E
C
T

PART TWO

Is Satan Real?

INVASION

How would you feel if you were to come home after work and there's a stranger sitting on your couch, eating your potato chips and watching your TV?

You would either leave out of fear or you would have that stranger removed--either voluntarily or involuntarily, but you wouldn't become friends with them.

It's time for the stranger to leave.
Not you.

The stranger in your house is Satan. What are you going to do about it?

It's time that you know and understand who he is and how he operates. There will be no more hiding from him. We've been given the keys to the Kingdom of heaven and we will use them against the forces of hell.

24

Satan

Satan doesn't want us to know that he exists. If he can keep us in the dark about who he is and how he operates, we will remain powerless and under his control. That should not be an option since we received Jesus as our Savior. Jesus conquered death, hell, and the grave so that we are no longer bound by the tyranny of Satan's rule over the earth.

Satan is real and his access in the world is not limited to non believers. In **John 8:44,** Jesus made this comment while being confronted by the religious sect, the Pharisees. This is what he said about them, "You belong to your father, the devil, and you want to carry out your father's desires. He was a murderer from the beginning, not holding to the truth, for there is no truth in him. When he lies, he speaks his native language, for he is a liar and the father of lies." Many of those that Jesus spoke of were priests, who understood well and taught the law, but their hearts were far from God.

Satan gains access to us by invitation. We invite him into our lives through our senses: what we see, hear, smell, taste and touch. He comes in when you're watching pornography. He comes into your life when you've eaten until you're full but he convinces you to eat more until it becomes gluttony. You just can't get enough. That's him.

It all begins subtly. It seems innocent. A little sin won't hurt anybody, right? But that's just the beginning and only on the surface. His invasion implodes from within us. Before we know anything, we have transformed into something so sinister that it's hard to come back from. Until the implosion topples everything over. Now, we're in a mess and need a way out.

SATAN

Once you're in his grasp, he won't let go without a fight. Everything that seemed so innocent has become an uncontrollable mess.

Your husband or wife stays out all night. You're exhausted. All you guys ever do now is fight.

Your children are out of control. And don't even mention all of the problems that you're facing

at work. You're tired from just thinking about it. To top it all off, you're beginning to question if you are good enough, whether or not anyone cares about you, or if life is even worth living anymore.

All of those problems are a result of Satan's presence. He really does come to kill, steal, and destroy.

What started so innocently has

become an aggressive attack on you and everything associated with you. You can hardly breathe from it's onslaught. You're smothering in bills you created from the enticement and lure of all the promises Satan made at your initial meeting. You're smoldering from the war with your children and the one in your own mind, until you're melting from the flaming fire of your own lustful desires. You can't just put this fire out on your own. You need help, but where can you go to get help fighting this opponent and come out ahead?

26

WHAT WE NEED TO KNOW

In situations like these, you need a Savior and not just any savior will do. You need one that has a track record of defeating the enemy that you're encountering.

Not only did Jesus defeat Satan, but when He conquered death and the grave, He brought out with Him other dead people who went back home to their families to show that Jesus had resurrection power on earth (Matthew 27:53).

The truth of the matter is that whether you decide that Jesus is your Savior or not, you will encounter problems in this life. These battles will either make or break you, either way, with Jesus on your side, even the breaking turns out for your good.

Whether you believe the evidence of Satan's existence or not, the aftermath of Satan's presence is felt everywhere today. You can cut evil with a knife in many places. Senseless murders are running rampant and no one is safe from thieves that break in to steal from us. Even driving on the highways or going to school has become a place of bloodshed, all in the wake of Satan's devices. He cunning and manipulative. He can't be trusted at all.

YOUR CHOICE

As a Christian, you are called to war. If you are a non believer in Jesus, you are a *prisoner of war*. Which do you prefer to be?

Read chapter 3: Make Peace with the Past in "The Way Out" companion book.

DISCUSSION QUESTIONS

Think through the questions before answering

1) Satan doesn't want us to know that he exists. Read Mark 4:15, Luke 13:6, Acts 26:18, and Luke 4:8. Discuss/Write your thoughts about who you think he is based on these scriptures.

2) Discussion Question: Do you know who Satan is? Explain your answer.

3) Discussion Question: Have you ever encountered him or his angels? How do you know? How did you get through that experience?

4) Discussion Question: Is it possible to go to hell although you've accepted Jesus as your Savior? If so, how? (Matthew 7:21-23)

PART THREE

Who was Lucifer?

Lucifer

When God named him, He intentionally pronounced who his character was to be. The name Lucifer literally means the bearer of light or the morning star.

Whether you call him Lucifer or Satan, he's not to be trusted. He's crafty, cunning, and can disguise himself in ways that many are deceived into believing that he can't be that bad. But he is.

He hates human beings. Why? Because God showers his love on us instead of him. He was once the apple of God's eye, but not anymore. He's been replaced by us. God's love for us inflames Satan's hatred of us.

And he's not alone. He is over a kingdom of angels that fell with him and their only mission is to cause us to leave the loving care of Father God.

30

WHO WAS LUCIFER?

He was a beautiful angel in heaven. In fact, he led the choir of angels in heaven. His body was created as an instrument of worship. As he walked, the sounds of melodious worship music were produced that brought God much glory, until vanity consumed him. It became all about him. His pride caused him to be thrown out because he elevated himself to God's status. He wanted to be worshipped although he was created to worship God.

Ezekiel 28 13-19 states:

You were the seal of perfection, Full of wisdom and perfect in beauty. You were in Eden, the garden of God; every precious stone was your covering: The sardius, topaz, and diamond, beryl, onyx, and jasper, sapphire, turquoise, and emerald with gold. The workmanship of your timbrels and pipes was prepared for you on the day you were created. You were the anointed cherub who covers; I established you; You were on the holy mountain of God; You walked back and forth in the midst of fiery stones. You were perfect in your ways from the day you were created, till iniquity was found in you. By the abundance of your trading you became filled with violence

within, and you sinned; Therefore, I cast you as a profane thing out of the mountain of God; And I destroyed you, O covering cherub, from the midst of the fiery stones. "Your heart was lifted up because of your beauty; you corrupted your wisdom for the sake of your splendor; I cast you to the ground, I laid you before kings, that they might gaze at you. You defiled your sanctuaries by the multitude of your iniquities, by the iniquity of your trading; Therefore, I brought fire from your midst; It devoured you, And I turned you to ashes upon the earth In the sight of all who saw you. All who knew you among the peoples are astonished at you; You have become a horror, and shall be no more forever." (NKJ Version)

He disguises himself as an Angel of Light. According to 2 Corinthians 11:14-15 "And no wonder, for even Satan disguises himself as an angel of light. So, it is no surprise if his servants, also, disguise themselves as servants of righteousness." That dispels the idea that he's red in color, has horns instead of ears, and has a tail. No. He disguises himself as someone appealing and lures you into his web where he casts a spell on you.

A QUICK NOTE

Satan is the father of lies and he wants to woo us away from our loving Father because he hates us. Don't fall prey to his empty words. Learn strategies to overcome him.

REFLECTIONS

Use this space to write down what you are hearing from the Holy Spirit as we complete this section. Everything you're experiencing is important to the process of transformation.

R
E
F
L
E
C
T

PART FOUR

Names for Satan in the Bible

NAMES FOR SATAN IN THE BIBLE

What's in a Name?

Then it was the inflection in his voice and the expression on his face as he said it that was hilarious.

I find it amazing, as I think back, that Flip Wilson, disguised as a woman married to a preacher would claim that the devil made him buy that dress. Wait for it. Yeah, I know.

All of that is amusing but true. But whether you call him the devil, Satan, or Lucifer, he's cunning, deceptive, and downright evil and only wants to confuse us about the importance of serving God.

When I was a child, I loved to watch the comedian, Flip Wilson on TV. As a part of his comedy sitcom, he would play the character of a woman named "Geraldine Jones." This character was supposed to be the wife of a preacher but she always claimed, "the devil made me do it." When she said this the audience and everyone in my home would laugh. It was funny because the dress was way too short which was inappropriate for a preacher's wife.

All through the bible, there is reference to who he is and his character. There are also references to different names that he is known by.

The following pages outlines the names that he's been given and the scripture references so that you see evidence of who he is, that he exists and that he is our enemy.

34

NAMES FOR SATAN

"And no wonder, for even Satan disguises himself as an angel of light. So, it is no surprise if his servants, also, disguise themselves as servants of righteousness." 2 Corinthians 11:14-15

Read Chapter 9: Face and Slay Your Giants in "The Way Out" companion book.

- [ ] Satan   II Corinthians 2:11

- [ ] the tempter   Matthew 4:3

- [ ] the devil   Matthew 4:5

- [ ] the enemy   Matthew 13:25, 39

- [ ] the wicked one   Matthew 13:38

- [ ] the dragon   Revelation 12:9

- [ ] the old serpent   Revelation 12:9

- [ ] that crooked serpent   Isaiah 27:1

- [ ] the accuser   Revelation 12:10

- [ ] the piercing serpent   Isaiah 27:1

- [ ] the deceiver   Revelation 12:9

- [ ] the adversary   I Peter 5:8

- [ ] the liar   John 8:44

NAMES FOR SATAN

"And no wonder, for even Satan disguises himself as an angel of light. So, it is no surprise if his servants, also, disguise themselves as servants of righteousness." 2 Corinthians 11:14-15

Read Chapter 9: Face and Slay Your Giants in "The Way Out" companion book.

- [ ] the father of lies   John 8:44

- [ ] the murderer   John 8:44

- [ ] the oppressor   Isaiah 14:4

- [ ] the day-star   Isaiah 14:12

- [ ] Lucifer   Isaiah 14:2

- [ ] the son of the morning   Isaiah 14:12

- [ ] the one that laid low the nations   Isaiah 14:12

- [ ] leviathan   Isaiah 27:1

- [ ] the dragon that is in the sea   Isaiah 27:1

- [ ] the anointed cherub   Ezekiel 28:14

- [ ] Beelzebub   Matthew 12:24

- [ ] Belial (which means "wickedness")   II Corinthians 6:15

- [ ] Apollyon (Greek for "destroyer")   Revelation 9:11

NAMES FOR SATAN

"And no wonder, for even Satan disguises himself as an angel of light. So, it is no surprise if his servants, also, disguise themselves as servants of righteousness." 2 Corinthians 11:14-15

Read Chapter 9: Face and Slay Your Giants in "The Way Out" companion book.

- [ ] Abaddon (Hebrew for "destruction")   Revelation 9:11

- [ ] angel of the bottomless pit   Revelation 9:11

- [ ] the prince of the world   John 14:30

- [ ] the prince of the power of the air   Ephesians 2:2

- [ ] the prince of the demons   Matthew 12:24

- [ ] the god of this world   II Corinthians 4:4

- [ ] an angel of light   II Corinthians 11:14

- [ ] the strong man   Luke 11:21

- [ ] the thief   John 10:10

- [ ] the wolf   John 10:12

- [ ] like a roaring lion   I Peter 5:8

- [ ] the spoiler   Isaiah 16:4

- [ ] the extortioner   Isaiah 16:4

KNOWLEDGE IS POWER

TO KNOW IS TO UNDERSTAND

"Knowledge is of no value unless you put it into practice."
— Anton Chekhov

of the devil until the Lord returns or we die.

Why do you need to know that Satan is real or what his names are? Because he is enemy number one to all humans, whether you confess Jesus as your Savior or not. It comes down to this, if you are a believer in Jesus, you are called to war. If you do not believe, you are a prisoner of war.

Satan is already defeated by Jesus. That's the part Jesus played in our salvation. Our part is repentance, receiving the Holy Spirit, and standing firm against the wiles

Ignorance is not bliss. Closing your eyes to the truth will not shelter you from the onslaught of Satan's tyrannical attacks because as I stated before, he hates ALL human beings. He uses the powerful to do his dirty work all over the world but if you choose not to exercise the authority that Jesus has given you because of what He did on the Cross, you are being deceived.

Believe on Jesus. Take up the keys that He has given you and use the power that you've been given to exercise dominion over all the power of the enemy. I promise you, all of heaven is backing you up as you make your decision to follow Christ.

38

PART FIVE

Satan rules a kingdom

SATAN RULES A KINGDOM

The Garden Experience

Because he couldn't rule in heaven, he took hold of the earth as it's ruler. But how? By invitation. Adam and Eve gave him permission to rule over them because of their own pride. It was deception through cunning persuasion that caused them to be put out of the Garden of Eden. Satan convinced them that they would be like God, if they ate of the Tree of Knowledge of good and evil. It came about through their acts of disobedience that changed their relationship with God. Notice that Satan, himself, approached them in this situation because he didn't have access to them before that. God walked with them daily in the Garden and that relationship was their hedge of protection.

FACT: SATAN IS REAL AND HE RULES A KINGDOM. ALTHOUGH A RULER, HE IS DEFEATED.

Permission Granted

That all changed, once he gained permission to be on earth. He set up his kingdom to rule over the earth by means of the second heaven. He rules over hemispheres, stratospheres, the airways, galaxies, and the atmosphere. In order to dominate, he uses his view from the sky as an advantage over us because we are earthbound.

SATAN RULES A KINGDOM

Isaiah 14:13-14 says, "You said in your heart, "I will ascend to the heavens; I will raise my throne above the stars of God; I will sit enthroned on the mount of assembly, on the utmost heights of Mount Zaphon. I will ascend above the tops of the clouds; I will make myself like the Most High." That's where he rules. Above the earth.

Who are his subjects? Fallen angels. One third of the original heavenly host of angels left heaven to follow after him. That speaks to his cunning nature and ability to convince anyone--even angels that once only followed the voice of God fell prey to his deception.

Satan has given them power as princes placed over territories in the earth. Under them, are other demons with lesser titles and are dispersed throughout the earth as directed. Points of reference in scripture are: Isaiah 14; Ezekiel 28; 1 John 5:19; Daniel 10; Ephesians 2:2; 2 Corinthians 4:4; Revelations 12:9, 13:7-9.

But we no longer have to be subjected to the oppression of Satan. Jesus came and broke the back of Satan and his kingdom. Jesus took back authority over death, hell, and the grave and gave us, who believe in Him, the keys to the Kingdom of heaven so that we destroy the works of the devil because he lives in us. There's no power without the Cross.

DO NOT BE DECIEVED

Satan is real and the demonic world is, too. We must be armed with the Truth of the Gospel in order to obtain and maintain our freedom given to us by Christ.

THE LIES OF SATAN

Read Ephesians 6:12, Ezekiel 28:11-17, Isaiah 14:12-15, also – Daniel 10ff, with emphasis on verses 20-21. The angel that was sent to give a message to Daniel referred to fighting against the prince of Persia & Greece." Those were principalities. Not people.

He will rule the earth if we don't rise up and take authority over him. Ref: 2 Cor. 4:4, John 14:30, John 12:31, John 16:11, Eph. 2:2, Ephesians 6:12, Colossians 2:15

He has placed princes over territories, regions, and nations. At their disposal, lower ranking demons report to these princes.

He has angels that followed him instead of God – Matthew 25:41

Satan doesn't want us to know he rules a kingdom

According to Ephesians 6:12, these princes are over principalities that includes territories, heads of state, office and authorities.

They are rulers of darkness –they will use people (such as a king or queen) who rule a country, area, group, etc. thereby ruling the subjects that they rule over.

According to Daniel 10:21-22, it took 2 angels to fight off the prince of Persia and Greece. This denotes authority over the region.

The common denominator to all disagreements that we have is more than likely caused by Satan's strategies. Always remember, the real enemy is not other people. It's Satan and he doesn't fight fair.

_____

_____

ACRONYMS FOR SATAN

Use this space to write down words that describe the nature of Satan. For each letter represented, think of words that start with that letter that most closely characterize who he is.

PART SIX

How Satan's kingdom Operates

"And I saw three loathsome spirits like frogs, leaping from the mouth of the dragon (Satan) and from the mouth of the beast (Antichrist, dictator) and from the mouth of the false prophet; for they are [actually] the spirits of demons, performing [miraculous] signs. And they go out to the kings of the entire inhabited earth, to gather them together for the war of the great day of God, the Almighty."

Revelations 16:13-14

Satan's kingdom

The kingdom of darkness didn't hit my home because I was one of them. No. They came against me as I began to understand who I am in Christ. I became a threat to Satan.

I was a singer and I studied music all of my life. That is the area that I had in common with Satan. Therefore, I should've been on his side and early on, I was. I wanted to sing for the world because it offered so many benefits.

I wanted to be the next Aretha Franklin. But the church that I grew up in and my family frowned upon the lifestyle that came along with the bright lights of the music industry so I backed down from all of the offers to make my name great.

I watched all of my friends dive head first into the industry and I also saw the dead end that was produced from their hot pursuit of fame and fortune. I didn't know it then, but that's exactly what happens when you follow what seems to be innocent. Those beds of roses are hiding the thorns that you encounter as you lay down in them. They cut you and they mar you for life, if you let them.

How Satan's Kingdom Works

Satan cunningly comes into our lives through our own desires and weaknesses. He uses our desire for power, our sexual appetite, lack of identity, or any number of things that feed our narcissistic nature to lure us into his tangled web where, once hooked we don't see a way out. He's amused by our ignorance and takes advantage of it by fostering a display of promises that he never intends to make good on.

He knows the road that he has led us on will lead to destruction. That was his plan all along. To lead us away from God and turning our allegiance to him.

He accomplishes his mission through the many princes that he has placed over territories, regions, and domains. His kingdom is made up of thousands of fallen angels. In fact, when he was thrown out of heaven, he took one-third of the angels and made them rulers over nations. Under them are demonic forces that roam the earth looking for those that they can devour.

This was demonstrated as written in Daniel 10:12-13 where the angel that Daniel encountered told him that he was delayed from coming to him because of the prince of Persia. This refers to ruling demons that were over the territory of Persia that fought the angel Michael and the messenger that came to deliver God's message to Daniel. These demonic forces were afraid of the message

that would be delivered and exercised their authority over the air to prevent them, however unsuccessfully as it turned out to be.

These demonic princes devise strategies to pull us toward people, places, and things that will lead us to destruction. They use their advantage of being over the air to observe us so that they know what makes us tick.

While most of us are sleeping they work Satan's plan. That's why we find so many criminal activities occurring during the night.

They are at home in the darkness so they are definitely opposed to being exposed to the light, which is the knowledge of who they are because it could be the end of their reign.

Whether it is today, tomorrow, or years from now, their time will end as possessors of the earth. But their time spent working against you can end right now. If you take action to learn who they are and devise biblical strategies of spiritual warfare, you, too will overcome their attempts to destroy your relationship with God.

The next set of pages outlines how Satan works against us with examples and scripture references so that you have biblical evidence of what we claim to be true. As we go over this material, reflect on how these same things may have happened in your own life.

A QUICK NOTE

"I have given you authority to trample on snakes and scorpions and to overcome all the power of the enemy; nothing will harm you." Luke 10:19

THE OPERATION OF SATAN'S KINGDOM

SHIPWRECKS

He shipwrecks your faith by slandering God which casts doubt about God's goodness. (Genesis 3:4-5).

TEMPTS

He tempts you with self-righteousness to deceive others in order to create, or maintain, the impression that you're more spiritual. (Acts 5:3; John 8:44).

CORRUPTS

He corrupts the mind to steer you away from the simplicity of Christ and His gospel. (2 Corinthians 11:3).

THE OPERATION OF SATAN'S KINGDOM

SEIZES

He snatches the Word of God out of the hearts of people and chokes out their faith in God. (1 Thess. 2:18, 3:5, Matthew 13:19).

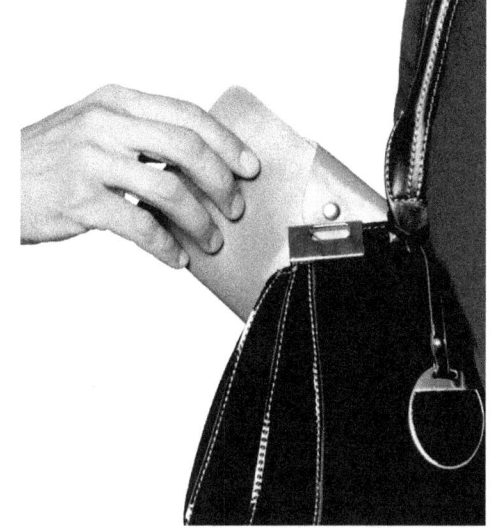

WRESTLES

He wrestles with you, fighting against your progress in Christ (Ephesians 6:12).

SEXUAL IMMORALITY

He tempts you to commit sexual immorality against your spouse as a result of neglecting the sacred nature of your marriage. (1 Corinthians 7:5).

THE OPERATION OF SATAN'S KINGDOM

HARASSES

He harasses you with all forms of fleshly affliction (2 Corinthians 12:7).

BLINDS

He blinds the mind of you and your unsaved loved ones from seeing the Truth. (2 Corinthians 4:4).

BONDAGE

He may keep your unsaved acquaintances in bondage to sins that hinder them from coming to God. (Galatians 4:8).

THE OPERATION OF SATAN'S KINGDOM

INFLICTS

He may inflict you with physical disease. (Luke 13:16; Job 2:7).

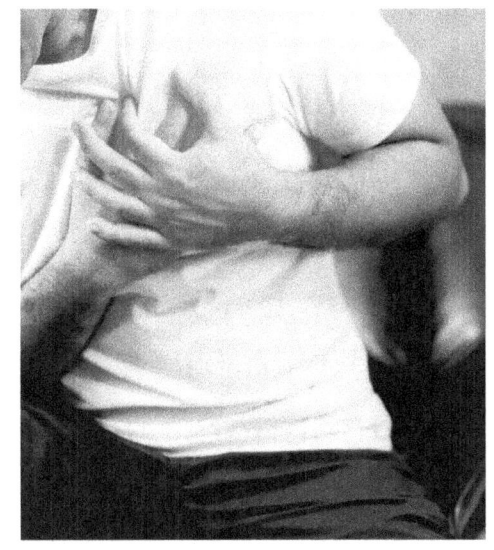

DESTROYS

He wants to kill you, but he doesn't have the power to. (Ps 106: 37; John 8:44, 1 John 3:12).

INVADES

He may send counterfeit Christians, or his followers within your houses of worship in order to deceive and create disunity. (Matthew 13:38-39; 2 Corinthians 11:13-15.)

THE OPERATION OF SATAN'S KINGDOM

LEAD YOU ASTRAY

He may lead you to compromise your religious beliefs by causing you to entertain false doctrine and its teachers. (1 Timothy 4:1-3).

PERSECUTES

He may persecute you for your godliness. (Revelations 2:10).

EVIL INFLUENCE

He may tempt you to do evil (Matthew 4:1; 1 Thessalonians 3:5).

THE OPERATION OF SATAN'S KINGDOM

PRIDE

He prowls about seeking to capture and destroy you, chiefly through pride (1 Peter 5:6-8.)

SLANDERS

He slanders you and your name before God in heaven. (Revelations 12:10).

ATTACKS

He asks God for permission to sift you through concentrated attacks and temptations. (Luke 22:31).

THE OPERATION OF SATAN'S KINGDOM

CONFUSES

He uses the power of suggestion to move you away from the will of God (Matt 16 21 23).

DISCOURAGES

He tries to cripple your effectiveness through confusion, discouragement, and despair (2 Corinthians 4:8-9).

WAGES WAR

He wages a war in our minds. (Proverbs 16:27-29).

THE OPERATION OF SATAN'S KINGDOM

He bargains with you.

He works within.

He even comforts your bad behavior.

He's cunning and taunts you day and night.

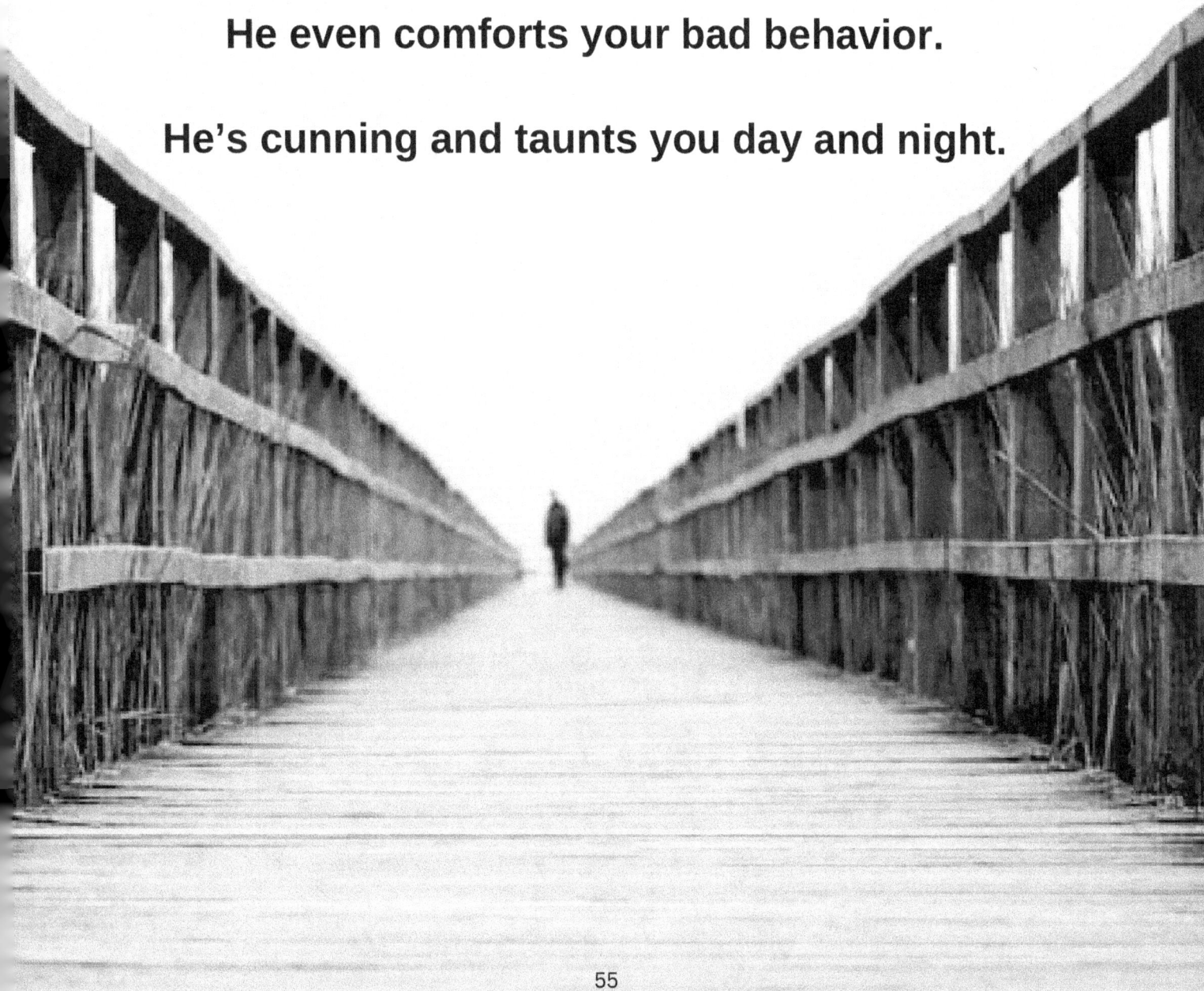

THE OPERATION OF SATAN'S KINGDOM

- He's crafty in designing opportunities that look like God did it.

- He causes some sickness and disease. (Luke 13:16, Acts 10:38)

- He may perform miracles through signs and wonders.
- (2 Thessalonians 2:9, Matthew 24:24, Matthew 7:22-23).

- He makes suggestions that on the surface look innocent, but you find your circumstances end up being wrecked by it.

REFLECTIONS

Use this space to write down what you are hearing from the Holy Spirit as we complete this section. Everything you're experiencing is important to the process of transformation.

R
E
F
L
E
C
T

PART SEVEN

The Disguise

THE DISGUISE

Hidden Agendas

Have you ever had someone dislike you so much that they would disguise themselves as **you** in order to make you look bad? I once had a manager, who was formerly my peer at another company, that asked me to join her at the new company that she was going to. I quickly accepted. We were friends and I felt that we would make a difference together.

After starting there, we found out that the company had a lot of internal problems that caused their customers to experience extreme wait times for approvals and closings. When the corporate office came to meet with us regarding the problems, I made a suggestion that could improve our turnaround times and upper management decided to implement them.

BE ALERT. EVERYTHING IS NOT WHAT IT APPEARS TO BE. STAY FOCUSED ON JESUS ALONE.

Identity Uncovered

Little did I know that my manager didn't like that I was noticed by upper management and she began to do whatever she could to make me look bad. In fact, I didn't know it at the time, but she had started keeping a file of my mistakes so that she could build a case to fire me. All the while that she's working behind my back to discredit

REMOVING THE VEIL

me, I had no knowledge of what she was doing.

But one day, she was out sick and I had to cover for her. In doing so, I had to review and sign off on loan conditions in order for loans to close in a timely manner. I reviewed the first file and noticed the name of the customer. I had denied that file. I went back to my files, because I kept a record of everything I did. It's called covering yourself, right? In my files, I found the denial and my reasons for the denial.

I came to the second, third, and fourth files and they were all files that I had denied previously. Two of them, still had my name on them as the underwriter. What was she up to? I was fuming. Who would do such a thing, especially in light of our "so called" friendship?

I called our corporate office to tell them what I found and wanted to know what I needed to do about those files that should have been denied but were ready to go to closing? The executive vice president told me that they had received notification of errors I had made because my manager had been building a file against me with all of my so-called mistakes. I was in disbelief. I thought we were good friends, not just work buddies. How did I miss this?

That's just the way that Satan works. He starts out acting like a friend, but he's our arch enemy. He entices us to leave the comfort of our Savior. Blinding us from the Truth, he prances around us as if we're buddies, but he's a fraud.

In his disguise, he makes it seem that God is the villain. He tells us that God is the one that caused all the troubles in the world, not him. With every event that occurs in our lives and in the world, he builds up a case against God that says God is the one doing all the damage that we see.

Yet, if we come a little closer, observing the real evidence, we see that God is not the perpetrator of all things evil. Satan is the one. He planned his dirt before we ever saw him coming. He doesn't like us. He's just pretending to be our friend in order to take us down to the pit of hell with him.

Misery loves company. But don't sit with him as he taunts us. He's cunning and is as slick as molasses, but there's nothing sweet about him.

In the following pages, we will uncover his disguise so that you get to see him for who he really is. The scripture references will give evidence that he's been this way since the beginning of time. Nothing's changed.

A QUICK NOTE

Light belongs in darkness for the light illuminates the Truth and lies are exposed. After that, the only remnant of darkness that remains are the shadows hiding behind objects. Come into the light because that's where you belong.

Read chapter 5: Clean House in "The Way Out" companion book.

60

SATAN'S DISGUISE

1 NOT ALL POWERFUL

- Satan doesn't want us to know that he is not all-powerful – Luke 10:18-20, Revelations 12:7-9, 2 Peter 2:4, 1 John 3:8, Romans 16:20

2 NOT ALL KNOWING

- Satan doesn't want us to know that he is not all-knowing (Omniscient) – Job 1:7

3 KNOWS THE WORD OF GOD

- Satan doesn't want us to know how he uses the Word of God to entrap us – Matthew 4 (tempting Jesus).

4 IS NOT OMNIPRESENT

- Satan doesn't want us to know that he cannot be everywhere all at once (Omnipresent)– 1 Peter 5:8, Job 1:6-7, Matthew 4:3, John 14:30

5 HIS TIME IS UP

- Satan doesn't want us to know that he doesn't have much time left – Romans 16:20

6 HE'S A DEFEATED FOE

- Satan doesn't want us to know that he's already defeated – Colossians 2:15, Hebrews 2:14-15, John 16:1

THE DISGUISE

Satan doesn't want us to know we're free. Read 2 Corinthians 3:17, John 8:36, Ephesians 3:12, Romans 6:22, 1 Peter 2:16, and John 8:32-36. We are:

- Free to choose – Acts 26:18, Ephesians 4:27

- Free to live as citizens of Heaven –John 14:2, Philippians 3:20, Luke 22:29-30, Ephesians 2:19, 1 Peter 1:4, Revelation 21:2

- Free from the cares of this world – Luke 12:22-31

- Free from the power of death – Hebrews 2:14-15

- Free to love – Galatians 5:13-14

- Free to forgive – Acts 13:38-39, Romans 8:1-4, Hebrews 9:14

- Free from sin – Galatians 5:1, Luke 4:18

DISCUSSION QUESTIONS

Think through the questions before answering

1) Discussion Question: Before going through this workbook, did you believe that Satan was real? What do you believe now?

2) Discussion Question: Do you believe in God? Why or why not?

3) Discussion Question: Do you believe that Jesus died for you, rose up out of the grave and is alive today? Is He your Savior?

4) Discussion Question: Is hell a real place? Is heaven a real place?

5) Discussion Question: Do you know where you're going when you die? What do you think happens after death?

EXPRESSIONS

Capture your thoughts as we work through this material. What are you hearing from the Holy Spirit? Write it down so that it packs a punch in who you become. This process is vital to your transformation.

PART EIGHT

Fake Identity

FAKE IDENTITY

When All Else Fails, Fake It

I once had a tenant that was caught stealing identities. Not just one, and not just two, but multiple identities. She had only been in the property for six to seven months when I received a call from a bank claiming that they needed to get payment back from us because of a fraudulent transaction. When I found out who it was, I was in disbelief. The company that did the background check showed an impeccable history but with this news, I went back to double check their work. When I did, I did a name check in every place she claimed to have lived and I was appalled at what I found. She had a criminal record a mile long and had a number of aliases. How did they miss this? She used a fake social security number.

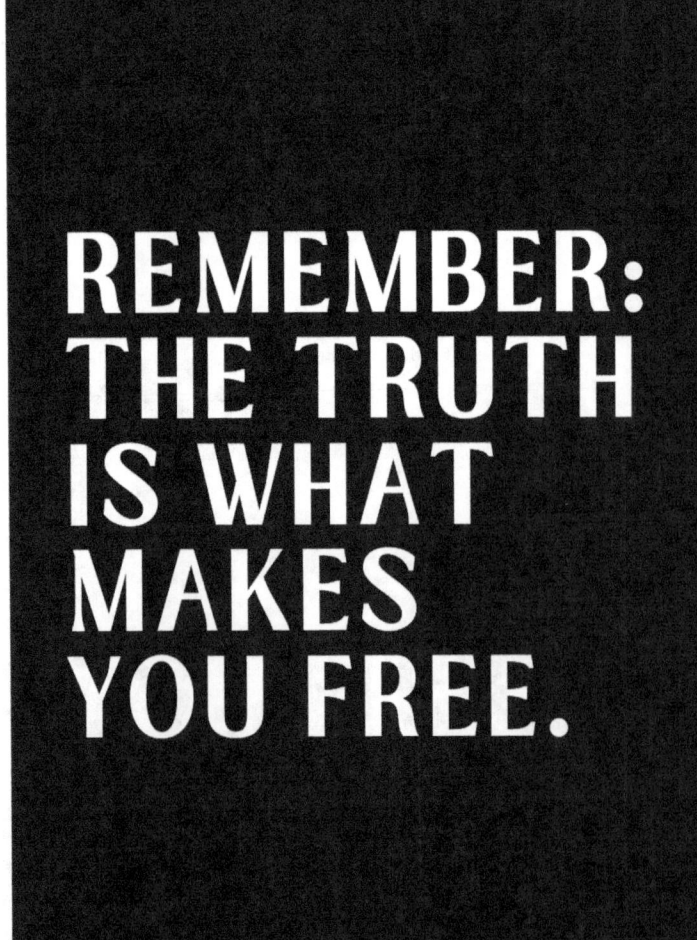

REMEMBER: THE TRUTH IS WHAT MAKES YOU FREE.

Who Are You?

Fake identity has become more and more of a problem in recent times. Some of it is due to the rise of social media and people feeling the need to embellish who they are and the stories they tell because they need more "likes." Who they really are is not good enough to cross the threshold of the numbers they need to become an influencer.

66

FAKE IDENTITY

Without the likes, they become depressed. It's an on the surface existence where no one is allowed into their inner circle. They alienate themselves from other people out of fear that their true identity will be discovered.

Their house of cards comes tumbling down when the first lie is uncovered. Then they go into hiding. This is where Satan loves for us to end up at. A mind that is threatened by the truth is ripe for destruction.

The truth illuminates their fears. Everyone can see they're an imposter. A phony. It's hard to recover a life after this type of exposure.

This is the place where people want to commit suicide. They feel that life is no longer worth living. They become alcoholics to escape their misery. Life wasn't supposed to be like this. But it all started with the need to be more than they were. Telling a lie seemed more appealing than the truth but in the end the truth will always come to the surface.

NO MORE FAKE ID'S

"Then Jesus said, 'Come to me, all of you who are weary and carry heavy burdens, and I will give you rest. Take my yoke upon you. Let me teach you, because I am humble and gentle at heart, and you will find rest for your souls.'"
Matthew 11:28-29

FAKE IDENTITY

WHO'S RESPONSIBLE?

Identity is a construct. Someone, somewhere along the way, spoke over your life, and told you who you would become. It's time to tear down that building and construct a new one on the right foundation.

REFLECTIONS

Use this space to write down what you are hearing from the Holy Spirit as we complete this section. Everything you're experiencing is important to the process of transformation.

R
E
F
L
E
C
T

PART NINE

Signs of Fake Identity

SIGNS OF FAKE IDENTITY

Read chapter 4: Feeling Stuck? Let It Go in "The Way Out" companion book.

THE SOURCE

When you look at yourself in the mirror, what do you see? Tell me, what emotions surface as you gaze upon your face? Start by moving from your eyes to your nose, your mouth, and even your skin tone. What do you see? As you do this and think about it, whose voice do you hear? Is it a family member that was downright mean to you as a child because of their own misplaced identity issues? Or were you molested as a child and no one came to rescue you? Who was it that you lived all of your life trying to measure up to? Do they even realize what they did to you?

COMING CLEAN

In order to come clean, you must recognize the signs of fake identity and the root cause of it. This requires you to be transparent with everyone, including yourself. Hiding is what brought you to this place, so freedom can only be found and realized when you tell the truth. Sit with that for a moment. What is the truth? What or who made you think the truth wasn't good enough?

SIGNS OF FAKE IDENTITY

How do I know so much about this? I, too, struggled with identity. I didn't feel that I measured up either. I looked around at my family and friends and I felt that who I was paled in comparison to them. So I began lying. I started at an early age embellishing the truth of my existence. Without blinking an eye, I made up stories to color my life in such a way that everyone was impressed. That is until the first lie was peeled back and exposed. Then I became a ghost. I disappeared.

Until I met the Holy Spirit and without judgment, He gently started cleaning out my spiritual closet. All the lies Satan convinced me of that led me to a life of lies and made up realities had to be undone. The Holy Spirit didn't do the work alone. He led me to the path, but it was my internal work to do and no one else.

Maya Angelou made the statement, "when you get, give, and when you learn, teach." That's the burning passion with which I write this material. I know what it feels like to hide behind fake identities but I also know the freedom that I found in Christ alone. It wasn't until I let go of those fake narratives that I held onto so dearly that all those burdens were lifted off of me.

IT'S YOUR TIME

Confess those things that cause you to take on fake or alternate identities. It's in your acknowledgement of where you've been that you can be set free.

SIGNS OF FAKE IDENTITY

There are times when you need help seeing the signs of what causes you to struggle with identity. The following list is a roadmap that represents the journey to the end results of fake identity. As we discuss them, don't hesitate or deny any of them that you know you struggle with. The purpose of this exercise is to come clean so that you can become free.

MILESTONE 1

You change who you are based on what others think.

MILESTONE 2

You change based on your environment.

MILESTONE 3

You have shallow or superficial relationships (i.e., only social media friends) that are "surface only."

MILESTONE 4

You display radical changes in your opinion based on external factors.

MILESTONE 5

Your relationships make or break you.

SIGNS OF FAKE IDENTITY

There are times when you need help seeing the signs of what causes you to struggle with identity. The following list is a roadmap that represents the journey to the end results of fake identity. As we discuss them, don't hesitate or deny any of them that you know you struggle with. The purpose of this exercise is to come clean so that you can become free.

MILESTONE 6

You don't know your worth. You've become like a spiritual "Bag Lady" filing for bankruptcy when you have a bankroll sitting in the bank. You just don't know it's there for you.

MILESTONE 8

You're defined by what you have or possess. Your possessions own you instead of you owning your possessions.

MILESTONE 7

You know there's more to life than what you have but you don't have a clue how to get it.

MILESTONE 9

You have trust issues.

MILESTONE 10

You don't have purpose.

SIGNS OF FAKE IDENTITY

There are times when you need help seeing the signs of what causes you to struggle with identity. The following list is a roadmap that represents the journey to the end results of fake identity. As we discuss them, don't hesitate or deny any of them that you know you struggle with. The purpose of this exercise is to come clean so that you can become free.

MILESTONE 11

You feel aimless in your pursuits.

MILESTONE 12

You don't feel life is worth living.

MILESTONE 13

You try to make life's labels placed on you the definition of who you are.

MILESTONE 14

You've had thoughts of suicide, and maybe even attempted suicide.

MILESTONE 15

At the opposite end of the spectrum--you think too highly of yourself. You're puffed up.

IDENTITY CRISIS
Signs of Fake Identity

Do you identify with any of the signs of fake identity? If so, which of them is most prevalent for you? It's okay if you identify with more than one or with all of them. We've all struggled with identity at one point or another. This practice is to bring it to the surface so that the Holy Spirit can help you formulate your way out of it. This is a no judgment zone.

PART TEN

Examples of Identity Struggles

STRUGGLING WITH IDENTITY

Human Dilemma

We've devoted a lot of time in this material on identity because it's vitally important. Knowing who you are gives you real power, not an artificial sense of it. When you know who you are, you walk, talk, and act differently,

I believe that no matter who you are, where you live, or how much money you have, you have at some point or another struggled with your identity, in some form or fashion. That's because it's one of the number one ways that Satan tries to attack you. He even tried to assault Jesus's identity, while He was in the wilderness and after fasting for forty-days,

DON'T GIVE UP BECAUSE IT'S HARD. KEEP GOING. THE BEST IS STILL YET TO COME.

Biblical Examples

The bible is full of people, just like you and I, who struggled in their identity. Can you imagine what Eve must've felt like knowing she was the reason they were evicted from their home? Or what about Tamar, King David's daughter that was raped by her half-brother? Think about this as we dive into observing others with identity struggles.

BIBLE CHARACTERS THAT STRUGGLED WITH IDENTITY

Read chapter 8: The New You, in "The Way Out" companion book.

DECEIVED EVE – GENESIS 3

_____

_____

_____

DEPRESSED CAIN – GENESIS 4

_____

_____

_____

SCHEMING JACOB – GENESIS 25 – 32

_____

_____

_____

JOSEPH'S GUILTY BROTHERS – GENESIS 37 & 42-44

_____

_____

_____

BIBLE CHARACTERS THAT STRUGGLED WITH IDENTITY

Read chapter 8: The New You, in "The Way Out" companion book.

MOSES – EXODUS 2:10-15

_____

_____

_____

NAOMI, RUTH'S MOTHER IN LAW – RUTH 1-4

_____

_____

_____

SAUL - 1 SAMUEL 9:21 – THE LEAST OF ALL FAMILIES

_____

_____

_____

DAVID – 2 SAMUEL 11:2-27

_____

_____

_____

BIBLE CHARACTERS THAT STRUGGLED WITH IDENTITY

Read chapter 8: The New You, in "The Way Out" companion book.

JEREMIAH, THE WEEPING PROPHET – JEREMIAH 20:14, 18

_____

_____

RAPED TAMAR (KING DAVID'S DAUGHTER) – 2 SAMUEL 13

_____

_____

PROUD HAMAN – ESTHER 5:9-14

_____

_____

POMPOUS NAAMAN – 2 KINGS 5

_____

_____

BIBLE CHARACTERS THAT STRUGGLED WITH IDENTITY

Read chapter 8: The New You, in "The Way Out" companion book.

JABEZ – 1 CHRONICLES 4:9-10

_____

_____

_____

JOSIAH – 2 KINGS 22 – 23

_____

_____

_____

MONEY LOVING JUDAS - JOHN 12:6, JOHN 6:70, MATTHEW 26:15; 1 TIMOTHY 6:10

_____

_____

_____

SAUL BEFORE HE BECAME PAUL – ACTS 7:54-58, ACTS 8:1-3

_____

_____

_____

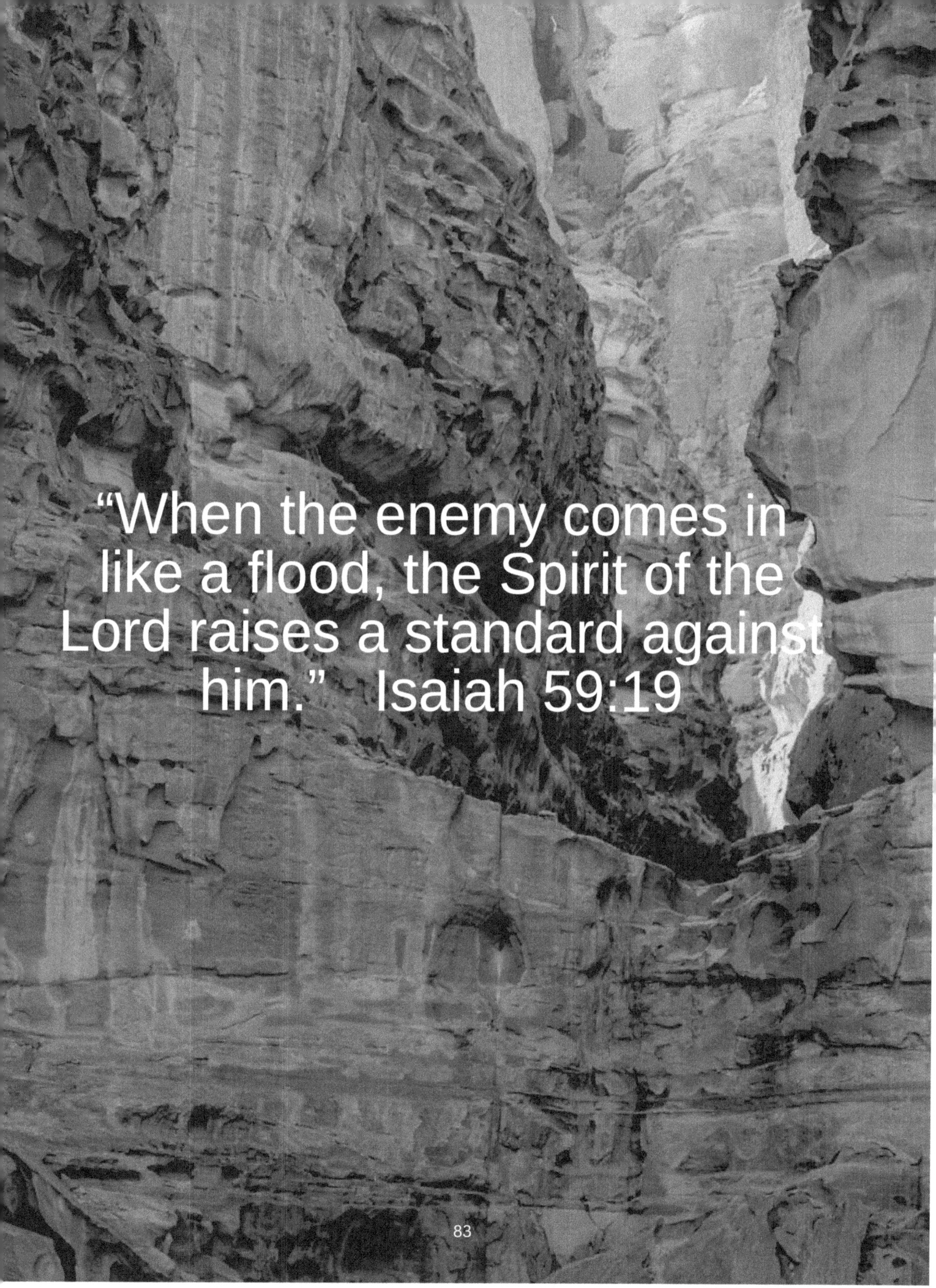

"When the enemy comes in like a flood, the Spirit of the Lord raises a standard against him."   Isaiah 59:19

SATAN ASSAULTS OUR IDENTITY

After understanding that Satan is real and how he operates, we must:

1. Know who we are

2. Know whose we are

3. Know where we are weak

YOUR KNOWLEDGE IS POWER

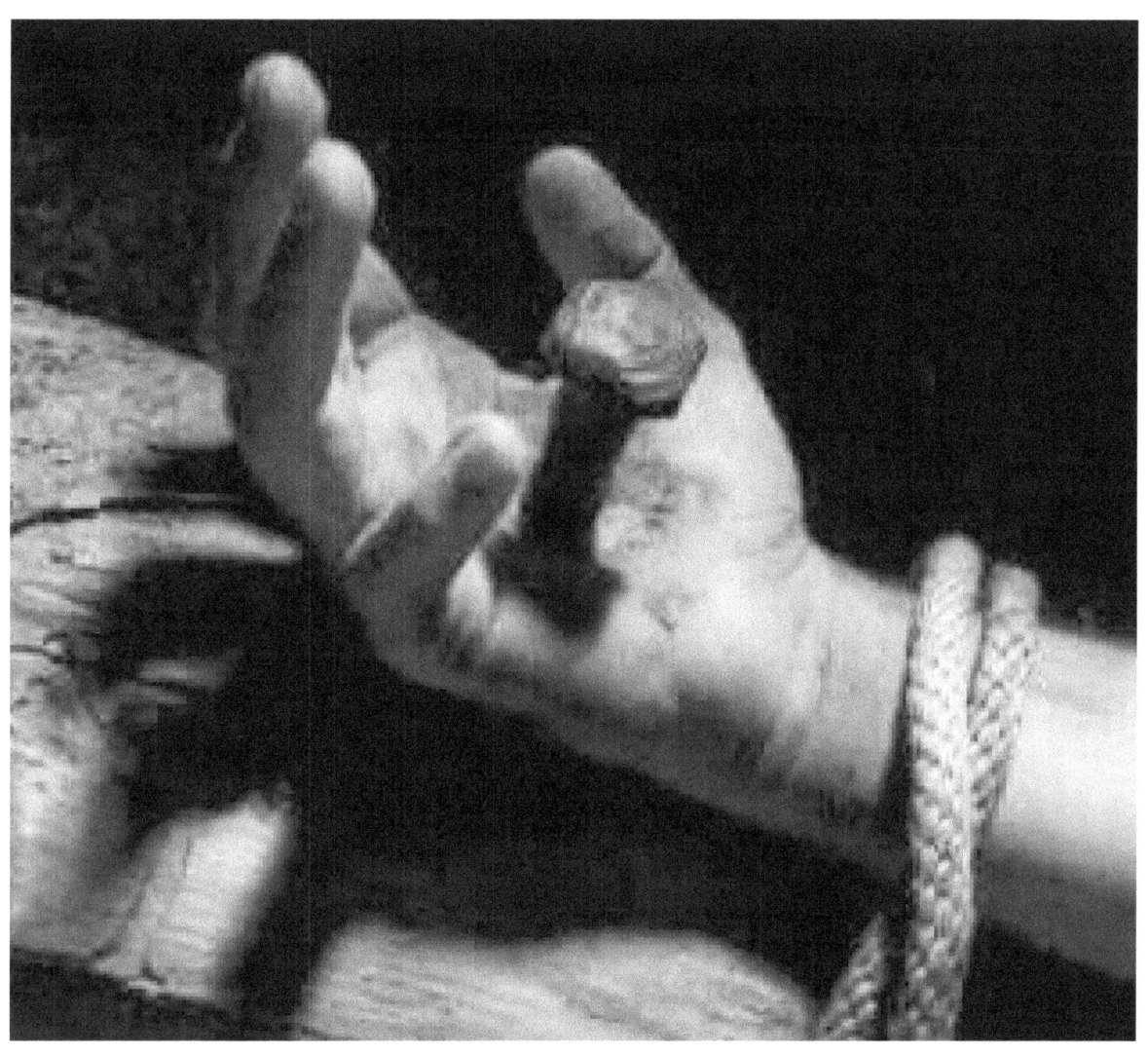

TAKE BACK YOUR IDENTITY

Stand on the Truth: that Jesus loves you and is your Savior. That's weapon #1. That's the reason for the fight. Satan hates that God lavishes His love on you now, instead of him. So, the main ingredient is knowing that you are truly loved by God. Never waiver from this truth. It is fundamental and foundational.

Love Always Leaves A Mark

IDENTITY STRUGGLES

Use this space to jot down ways in which you struggle with identity, whether it is that you think too highly of yourself or you think less of yourself than you ought to.

PART ELEVEN

Foundations of Identity

Who We Are

Then God said, "Let Us make man in Our image, according to Our likeness; let them have **dominion** over the fish of the sea, over the birds of the air, and over the cattle, over all the earth and over every creeping thing that creeps on the earth." Genesis 1:26 .

God made us in His image. But why? He had already created everything else by speaking them into existence. When He created the light, He hovered over it and spoke to the darkness and light appeared. God spoke to the land for it to produce all types of vegetation. He spoke into reality every other living thing, but when he created us, He gave of Himself. He breathed into man for him to become alive. There is no life in man without the breath of God.

The question is why would He do such a thing? So that we would have His essence to rule over all the other created things. When the need arose for other things to be created, the Creator that was breathed into man had the power to bring it into existence. Unfortunately, Satan came to destroy God's original plan of perfection by tempting Adam and Eve to sin against God. A part of their punishment was the loss of their home and separation from God.

By the sin of Adam, we became separated from God, but by the righteous, redeeming, and sacrificial acts of Jesus, we can be reconciled to Him; thereby, restoring God's plan for man to have dominion. It's only possible through Jesus the Christ because what He did, as the last and final sacrifice for our atonement, was to take back authority from Satan and give it to us.

Jesus didn't just come to earth to establish another religion. In fact, He was opposed to those considered highly religious because they worked twice as hard to keep those who needed God from Him. He came to establish His kingdom on earth. He is the seed of David who came to rule His kingdom forever (2 Samuel 7:12-16). The Church is that kingdom and we are citizens of it.

It is NOT a democracy. You can't vote on the laws, how the kingdom will function, or who will

The Foundations of the Kingdom

govern. In a kingdom, the King has absolute rule. He is sovereign. What does sovereignty mean? The Oxford Dictionary defines it as supreme power or authority. With His supreme power, God wrote all laws and determined how they are to be enforced. We are His subjects on earth because we are followers of Jesus. Therefore, we rule the earth on His behalf. We are *like* His enforcers. It is our job to ensure that God's laws are known and carried out.

What Jesus achieved on the Cross, is far greater than just giving us citizenship in His Kingdom. The Father calls us His children. He adopted us into His family. According to Ephesians 1:5 (NLT) "God decided in advance to adopt us into his own family by bringing us to himself through Jesus Christ. This is what he wanted to do, and it gave him great pleasure."

There are benefits, rights, and privileges to being in God's Royal family. A part of that is having dominion. But having and exercising dominion are two different things. To have a billion dollars in the bank is great, but if you never withdraw money from the account to use it, you never realize all the power that has been given to you. To have it is to use it.

The dominion that has been given to us through our Savior exceeds what was given to Adam in the beginning of time. We are now kings and priests (Revelations 1:6). What does that mean? It means that within us lies a ruler and the righteousness of God. As priests, we are afforded a relationship with the Father that is richer than the "behind the veil" access that the Levitical priests were given. We no longer need anyone else to go to God on our behalf. We can go to Him directly, and we don't have to fear His presence (Exodus 19:16-20). We call Him "Abba" as a term of endearment. God didn't only come near when Jesus entered the world, but as Jesus and the Father are One, we are one with Him. To have the Holy Spirit lead and guide us is evidence that we have a righteousness that is not our own. When we accept Jesus as our Lord and King and receive His Spirit living on the inside of us, we gain the authority we need to take back dominion from Satan. God wants us to rule while wearing the robe of righteousness given to us through the sacrificial acts of Jesus (Isaiah 61:10-11). That's the only way that true dominion is demonstrated.

This domination is exhibited when we use the keys of the kingdom that Jesus gave us.

A QUICK NOTE

"For unto us a Child is born, Unto us a Son is given; and **the government** will be upon His shoulder. And His name will be called Wonderful, Counselor, Mighty God, Everlasting Father, Prince of Peace. Of the increase of **His government and peace** there will be no end, Upon the throne of David and over His kingdom, to order it and establish it with judgment and justice from that time forward, even forever. The zeal of the Lord of hosts will perform this." Isaiah 9:6-7

Read chapter 7: No More Fake IDs in "The Way Out" companion book.

89

THE FOUNDATIONS OF THE KINGDOM

We now have the power to cause heaven to come to earth through what we decree. It's through binding and loosing as we are Holy Spirit led that God's Will is done on earth(Matthew 16:19).

That's the reason Satan's attacks against us are so fierce. He doesn't want us to know who we are and whose we are. And he definitely doesn't want us to use it against him, but that is exactly why Jesus came to earth in the first place. He came to destroy the works of the enemy (1 John 3:8).

But how can this be, when Jesus returned to heaven to be with the Father after His resurrection from the dead? His Spirit was given to us as a deposit of heaven to live in and guide us. Through this empowerment from heaven, we exercise righteous dominion in the earth.

The power is in our decree and agreement. According to 2 Corinthians 5:18-20, we are ambassadors for Christ. As such, we represent our heavenly home on earth. We have been sent into the world to ensure compliance with God's laws; therefore, we must decree God's Word to enforce them. When we do, heaven backs us up. That's what is meant by binding and loosing. Whatever we arrest here on earth, is also arrested in heaven. We work in concert or agreement with heaven in dispensing righteousness.

The following pages provide exercises for you to complete to help you unpack those old ideologies and help you reframe your future with the knowledge of your true identity found only in Christ. Your change begins here.

THE POWER OF YOUR DECREE

"Thou shalt also decree a thing, and it shall be established unto thee: and the light shall shine upon thy ways." Job 22:28

90

Foundations of Identity:

To build any building, you must begin with a firm foundation. To connect to this foundation of Identity, Read 1 Corinthians 3:11, Isaiah 28:16, 1 Peter 2:6, Matthew 7:24, 2 Timothy 2:19, 1 Samuel 2:2, Psalm 62:2, Psalm 118:22. Focus on the following that make up your foundation:

- Name

- Biological factors: Family/Parents/Siblings or None/Illegitimacy

- Environment: Country, Work, etc.

- Social Cognition

- Character

- Personality

- Ownership: Who's Your Daddy?

- Group Affiliation

MY SELF
portrait

Sometimes what others see is different from what we see. Color the left side how you think others see you. Color the right side how you see yourself.

My outer self | My Inner self

"FORGIVENESS SAYS YOU ARE GIVEN ANOTHER CHANCE TO MAKE A NEW BEGINNING."

"FORGIVENESS SAYS YOU ARE GIVEN ANOTHER CHANCE TO MAKE A NEW BEGINNING."

DESMOND TUTU

HIERARCHY OF
A New You

It's important to set the foundation for your new identity on the Truth. There will be no more lies about who you are and your value. Establish clear boundaries so that those who want to come to bring up your past or want to drag you back to being empty and broken have no platform to speak from. They are no longer welcome here. You can't feel sorry for them after you've done the work to clean out the garbage they left. *This is your new beginning.* It's a fresh start and everyone has to be clear about your new existence.

TRUST .... **TRUST GOD & THE PROCESS**

LOVE .... **LOVE GOD, YOURSELF & OTHERS**

TRUTH .... **JESUS IS YOUR SAVIOR**

THE 3 DIMENSIONS OF
Who You Are

These 3 aspects of who you are is important to understand as you construct a new life. It's vital that you see the connection.

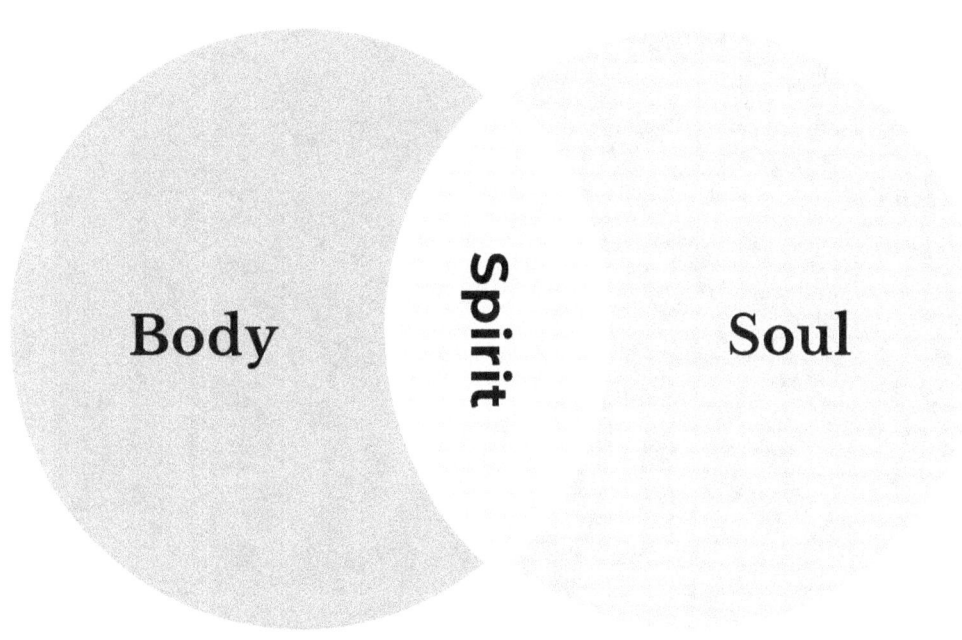

Body **Spirit** **Soul**

01 **THE BODY**
Within your body, resides your soul and your spirit. The choices you make for the body doesn't come from the body's decisions.

02 **THE SOUL**
The soul controls what the body does and it makes all decisions for it. The soul is where you experience the elements of life: what you see, smell, touch, hear, and taste.

03 **THE SPIRIT**
The spirit is where God wants to live in you but the choice is dependent on the soul choosing who it will follow. God doesn't want to dominate your life. He wants you to choose Him and He will send His Spirit to live in you, thereby helping the soul make better choices.

CHANGE

ROAD MAP FOR
Your Success

BE SPECIFIC. FROM YOUR VISUALIZATION, WHAT COMES TO MIND?

DON'T LEAVE OUT ANY DETAILS. MAKE THIS YOUR BREAKOUT YEAR WITH A WORKABLE PLAN.

WHO ARE THE PEOPLE, PLACES, OR THINGS CRITICAL TO THE PLAN?

HOW MUCH TIME WILL IT TAKE TO ACHIEVE? HOW WILL IT PLAY OUT IN REALITY?

THE PLAN FOR YOUR LIFE

IDENTIFY THE MEASURING TOOLS NEEDED TO MEASURE PROGRESS.

KEEP YOUR WHY AT THE CENTER OF YOUR PLAN. FORGET THE DISTRACTIONS. STAY FOCUSED.

BE INTENTIONAL IN ADDING OR DELETING RELATIONSHIPS. DEVELOP SOLID OR IMPROVE EXISTING RELATIONSHIPS

WHAT SKILLS DO YOU NEED TO GET WHERE YOU WANT TO BE?

EXPRESSIONS

Capture your thoughts as we work through this material. What are you hearing from the Holy Spirit? Write it down so that it packs a punch in who you become. This process is vital to your transformation.

Proverbs 23:7

"As a man thinks in his heart, so is he..."

PART TWELVE

Finding True Identity

FINDING TRUE IDENTITY

Know Your Rights

On a recent trip abroad, I purchased a service that gave me access to move through security faster than normal, but I forgot that I purchased it. I don't know if I forgot because of the number of days that I was traveling or just so that the magnitude of it would inspire writing this portion of the training, I don't know, but it moved me to share it with you.

Upon arriving at the airport, I proceeded to the security line, as usual, but when I got to the gate keeper that came into the line as I entered, she asked to see my boarding pass.

IT'S TIME FOR YOU TO STAND FIRM ON WHO YOU ARE AND WHOSE YOU ARE.

The Wait Is Over

Once I showed it to her, she pointed out that I had the right to the priority line with no wait. If she had not entered the line when she did, asking for boarding passes, I would have gone through a line that was five times as long as the priority one, although I had been given the privilege of having no wait time.

FINDING TRUE IDENTITY

It wasn't enough for me to have purchased this service without actually exercising my right to use it. It's the same with what we've been given because Jesus died for our sins. Christ's sacrifice wasn't only for the life to come, but it's for us right here and now. It gives us benefits that only come when we know who we are and whose we are.

When we know, everyone else will know and see the fruits of it. This comes from a firm foundation that we didn't set and no one else can do it for us. It's not fluid or wishy washy. No. It stands the test of time and will withstand any torrential storms that we may encounter in life.

The exercises that are to come next are similar to what the Holy Spirit had me to do when I struggled in my own identity because of life's blow by blow punch against me. One of the first and most consistent exercises that the Holy Spirit led me to do was after He would wake me at 3 am, He would tell me to go to the bathroom mirror, look at myself, gazing deeply into my own eyes and tell myself that "I love you, Lauraine." These exercises may seem mundane, but I promise you, they are oh, so impactful, so don't skip over any of it. It will work for your good. Trust the process.

IT'S TIME

Say goodbye to the old you because God has assigned you to do the work to produce His original plans that have your name written on them.

Read chapter 10: Get Out & Stay Out in "The Way Out" companion book.

FINDING TRUE IDENTITY

Zephaniah 3:17

BUILD – Construct by putting the parts or materials together over a period of time. First, you envision what you want & where you want to be, then you draw plans, buy the lot, perform perc tests, if septic is required for sanitation, purchase materials, hire professionals trained in construction, clear the lot of trees and debris, move excess dirt, dig out areas for the foundation to be poured, pour footings to stabilize the foundation, then you pour the foundation. Once the foundation has been poured, you wait for it to cure and firm up before you begin the process of framing. Inspections are performed at every stage of construction by local officials to ensure the integrity of construction quality.

YOU'RE GOING TO LIVE AGAIN!

Construction Map

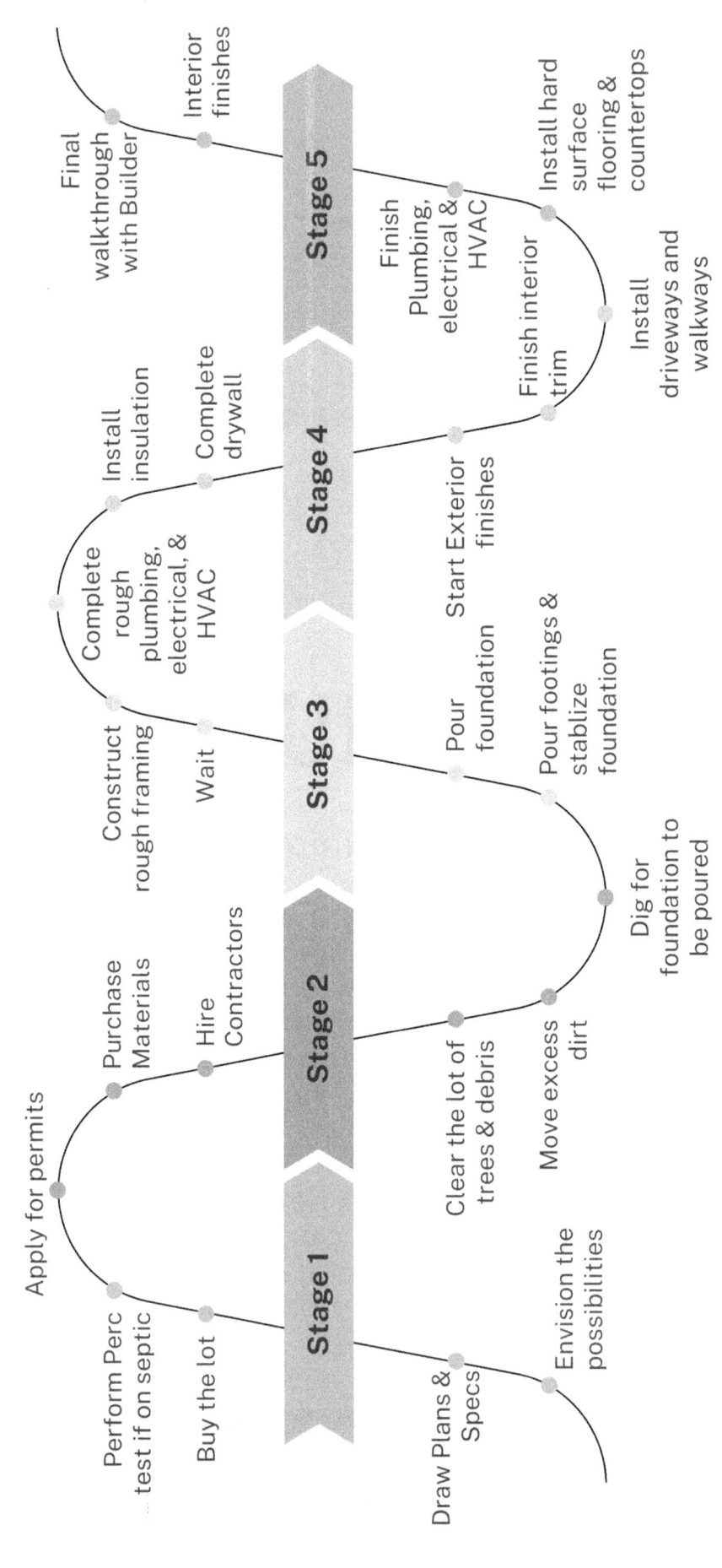

Stage 1 — Draw Plans & Specs, Envision the possibilities, Perform Perc test if on septic, Buy the lot, Apply for permits

Stage 2 — Purchase Materials, Hire Contractors, Clear the lot of trees & debris, Move excess dirt, Dig for foundation to be poured

Stage 3 — Construct rough framing, Wait, Complete rough plumbing, electrical, & HVAC, Pour foundation, Pour footings & stablize foundation

Stage 4 — Install insulation, Complete drywall, Start Exterior finishes

Stage 5 — Final walkthrough with Builder, Interior finishes, Finish Plumbing, electrical & HVAC, Finish interior trim, Install hard surface flooring & countertops, Install driveways and walkways

PLANNING FOR YOUR FUTURE

"Therefore if anyone is in Christ [that is, grafted in, joined to Him by faith in Him as Savior], he is a new creature [reborn and renewed by the Holy Spirit]; the old things [the previous moral and spiritual condition] have passed away. Behold, new things have come [because spiritual awakening brings a new life]." 2 Corinthians 5:17 AMP

VISION

- See the possibilities. Use the space on the Vision Board and be specific about where you are going.

- Perform a feasibility study. Crunch numbers, evaluate your history to envision your future self.

- Draw and design a potential plan. Absolutely nothing is impossible.

- What will this plan cost in time, education, and relationships?

PLANNING

- Study the Word of God.

- Accept the Holy Spirit as your guide, if you haven't already done so. How do you know? By the fruit you bear.

- Evaluate your current relationships. Will they help or hinder your growth?

- Unlearn old thoughts and patterns of behavior and turn to the new.

EXECUTION

- Find a spiritual mentor that will help you when times get tough. Preferably a prayer warrior.

- Join a body of believers, if you're not a part of one.

- If you belong to a church, decide on staying or leaving it.

- Establish new relationships with people aligned with where you are going.

PLANNING FOR YOUR FUTURE

"Therefore if anyone is in Christ [that is, grafted in, joined to Him by faith in Him as Savior], he is a new creature [reborn and renewed by the Holy Spirit]; the old things [the previous moral and spiritual condition] have passed away. Behold, new things have come [because spiritual awakening brings a new life]." 2 Corinthians 5:17 AMP

PERFORMANCE

- Become active at your place of worship but be careful not to become an idol worshipper of men or women in ministry. Idol worship, in any form is an abomination to God.

- Get equipped with strategic bible verses to stand on in times of testing and trouble. This comes from bible study.

- Exercise the gifts God has given you. Start with yourself and close family/friends where judgment is less offensive.

- Find balance between mind, body, and spirit so that you are not susceptible to attacks from the enemy. He looks for weaknesses so that he can take you out. Don't let him.

CLOSE / MOVING DAY

- Exercise dominion in the earth through your gifts and prayers. God is backing you up and Satan knows who you are now.

- Cooperate with the Holy Spirit to do the work of ministry that you and God have determined.

- Let go of the past and those that hurt you. This next season is bright so don't dim the light with the darkness of yesterday.

- Put on your running shoes because things are about to shift quickly. You don't have time to think about anything but to move with God as the Spirit leads you.

It starts with a Vision

travel

GOALS

....
....
....
....
....

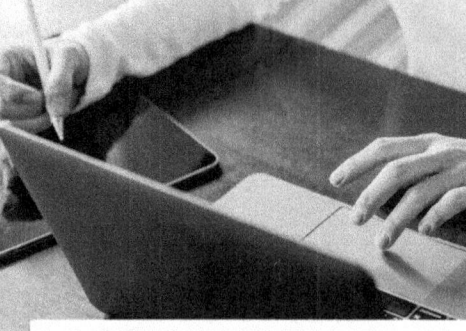

LIVING BY GOD'S DESIGN

CAREER

....
....
....
....
....

Spirituality

MONEY

....
....
....
....

VISION BOARD
worksheet
LIVING BY GOD'S DESIGN

PLANNING WORKSHEET

1. List what's important to you. Remember He chose you - Ephesians 1:3-7

2. Visualize where you want to grow to.

3. Plot a plan to recover from the past. What are the steps that you need to take?

4. What are the obstacles and rewards for change?

VISION WORKSHEET
Without a Vision, The People Perish

From Vision to Goal Setting

List out the people and the tools you need to execute your plan. Don't leave out any details. Drill down to the smallest of details. Everything is important to insuring the completion of this process.

VISION BOARD
Proclaim Your Purpose

WHAT DO YOU VALUE?

WHY IS THIS IMPORTANT?

HOW DO THESE VALUES DETERMINE YOUR PURPOSE?

WHO CAN HELP YOU?

ARE THERE OBSTACLES TO ACHIEVE YOUR PURPOSE?

BE SPECIFIC

SWOT ANALYSIS

STRENGTHS

WEAKNESSES

OPPORTUNITIES

THREATS

SWOT ANALYSIS

In general, having strength allows a person to perform tasks that require physical or mental effort, and it can also be a measure of a person's overall spiritual health and fitness.

STRENGTHS

WEAKNESSES

A weakness is a lack of strength or ability in a certain area. It can refer to a physical limitation, or it can refer to a personal characteristic or trait that makes it difficult for a person to succeed in a particular situation.

An opportunity is a chance or favorable set of circumstances that allows a person to do something or achieve something. Opportunities can arise in many different areas of life, such as work, education, or personal relationships.

OPPORTUNITIES

THREATS

A threat is a potential source of danger or harm. It can refer to a person, a group, an event, or a situation that has the potential to cause injury, damage, or loss.

CHANGE IS HERE

Change your thoughts and the words you speak will also change. Prayer, studying God's word, and joining a community of believers is essential to realizing this shift in mindset. The transformation that comes from renewing your mind with specific, biblical knowledge that causes you to make a decision is priceless.

YOU CAN'T STAY IN A DRY PLACE WHEN YOU'VE BEEN WATERED WITH THE WORD OF GOD.

God's Words Spoken Over You...

YOU ARE
WORTHY

I GIVE YOU
PEACE

I WILL
ALWAYS
LOVE YOU

YOU ARE
SAVED

WHAT GOD
SAYS
ABOUT
YOU

YOU ARE
FORGIVEN

YOU ARE
CHOSEN

YOU ARE
MY CHILD

YOU ARE
COMPLETE
IN ME

Embrace the words that God speaks about you and forget the words spoken over you from the past. These are the only words that matter now. Take hold of your future self by believing God's Words. Look in the mirror as you speak these things over yourself. God wants you to be whole and complete in Him. Take time to do this exercise everyday.

DAILY AFFIRMATIONS

As you step into the miracle of this new season, speak life over yourself. Declare these words every day and watch your transformation unfold before your eyes.

Read chapter 6: Pray..Wait...Hear in "The Way Out" companion book.

1) I am a child of God. (John 1:12, 1 John 3:1,2)

2) I am loved. (1 John 4:10)

3) I am forgiven. (1 John 2:12)

4) I am born again. (1 Peter 1:23)

5) I have new life. (1 John 5:12)

6) I am healed. (Isaiah 53:5)

7) I am the salt of the earth (Matthew 5:13)

8) I am the light of the world. (Matthew 5:14)

9) I am blameless and free from accusations. (Colossians 1:22)

10) Christ lives in me. (Colossians 1:27)

11) I am firmly rooted in Christ. (Colossians 2:7)

12) I am complete in Christ. (Colossians 2:10)

13) I am spiritually circumcised. My sinful nature is cutoff. (Colossians 2:11)

14) I am buried, raised, and made alive with Christ. (Colossians 2:12,13)

15) I died with Christ and I have been raised up with Him. My life is now hidden with Christ in God. Christ is now my life. (Colossians 1:1-4)

16) I am an expression of the life of Christ because He is my life. (Colossians 3:4)

17) I am chosen by God, holy and dearly loved. (Col. 3:12; 1 Thess. 1:4)

DAILY AFFIRMATIONS

As you step into the miracle of this new season, speak life over yourself. Declare these words every day and watch your transformation unfold before your eyes.

Read chapter 6: Pray..Wait...Hear in "The Way Out" companion book.

18) I am a child of light and not of darkness. (1 Thessalonians 5:5)

19) I have been given a spirit of power, love, and self-discipline. (2 Timothy 1:7)

20) I am saved and set apart for God's work. (2 Timothy 1:9; Titus 3:5)

21) Jesus is not ashamed to call me brother/sister. (Hebrews 2:11)

22) I am pursuing my heavenly calling. (Hebrews 3:1)

23) I come to God with boldness, freedom, and confidence. (Ephesians 3:12, Hebrews 4:16)

24) I am being built up in Christ as a spiritual house. (1 Peter 2:5)

25) I am a chosen generation, a royal priesthood, a holy nation, God's own possession. (1 Peter 2:9-10)

26) I hold onto God's Promises for they are yes and amen. (2 Corinthians 1:20)

27) I am anointed by God. (1 John 2:27)

28) I am like Christ. (1 John 4:10)

29) I am born of God and Satan cannot touch me. (1 John 5:8)

30) I am redeemed and forgiven. My debt is cancelled. (Revelation 5:9; Colossians 1:14)

31) I am commissioned to make disciples. (Matthew 28:19,20)

32) I hear Christ's voice and obey Him. (John 10:27)

33) I am saved. (1 John 5:13, Acts 16:31)

DAILY AFFIRMATIONS

As you step into the miracle of this new season, speak life over yourself. Declare these words every day and watch your transformation unfold before your eyes.

Read chapter 6: Pray..Wait...Hear in "The Way Out" companion book.

34) I have peace. (John 14:27)

35) I am part of the true vine, a carrier of Christ's life. (John 15:1,5)

36) I am clean. (John 15:3)

37) I am a friend of Christ. (John 15:15)

38) I am chosen by Christ to bear His fruit. (John 15:16)

39) I have been given God's glory. (John 17:22)

40) I am justified...completely forgiven and made righteous. (Romans 5:1)

41) I died with Christ and sin no longer rules me. (Romans 6:6)

42) I am a servant of righteousness. (Romans 6:18)

43) I am free from sin and receive the gift of eternal life from God. (Romans 6:22)

44) I am free forever from condemnation. (Romans 8:1)

45) I am a child of God and one in Christ. (Galatians 3:28, Romans 8:14)

46) I am a joint heir with Christ to God's Promise. (Romans 8:17; Galatians 4:6-7)

47) I am more than a conqueror through Christ, who loves me. (Romans 8:37)

48) I have faith in God. (Romans 12:3)

49) I am sanctified. (1 Corinthians 1:2)

50) I have grace through Christ Jesus. (Ephesians 2:8)

51) I am placed into Christ, by God's doing. (1 Corinthians 1:30)

52) I have the Spirit of God living in me showing me what God has for me. (1 Corinthians 2:12)

DAILY AFFIRMATIONS

As you step into the miracle of this new season, speak life over yourself. Declare these words every day and watch your transformation unfold before your eyes.

Read chapter 6: Pray..Wait...Hear in "The Way Out" companion book.

53) I have the mind of Christ. (1 Corinthians 2:16)

54) I am a dwelling place for God's Spirit. (1 Corinthians 3:16; 6:19)

55) I am an expression of God's Love. (1 John 4:7-11)

56) I am bought with a precious price; I am not my own; I belong to God. (1 Corinthians 6:19-20; 7:23)

57) I am called out by God. (1 Corinthians 7:17)

58) I am a member of Christ's Body. (1 Corinthians 12:27; Eph. 5:30)

59) I am victorious over every obstacle I face through Jesus Christ. (1 Corinthians 15:57)

60) I have been established, anointed and sealed by God in Christ. (2 Corinthians 1:21-22)

61) I am led by God in triumph. (2 Corinthians 2:14)

62) I am a sweet fragrance to God because of Christ. (2 Cor. 2:15)

63) I am changed into Christ's likeness. (2 Corinthians 3:18)

64) I am crucified with Christ, and I no longer live, but Christ lives in me. This life I live is His. (Galatians 2:20)

65) I reign with Christ. (2 Timothy 2:12; Romans 5:17)

66) I no longer live for myself, but for Christ. (2 Corinthians 5:14-15)

67) I am a new creation. (2 Corinthians 5:17)

68) I am reconciled to God (2 Corinthians 5:18-19)

69) I am a minister of reconciliation. (2 Corinthians 5:18-19)

70) I am the righteousness of God. (2 Corinthians 5:21; Ephesians 2:24)

DAILY AFFIRMATIONS

As you step into the miracle of this new season, speak life over yourself. Declare these words every day and watch your transformation unfold before your eyes.

Read chapter 6: Pray..Wait...Hear in "The Way Out" companion book.

71) I have strength instead of weakness. (2 Corinthians 12:10)

72) I am Abraham's seed...an heir to the Promise. (Galatians 3:29)

73) I am a saint. (Ephesians 1:1, Corinthians 1:2, Philippians 1:1, Colossians 1:2)

74) I am blessed with all spiritual blessings. (Ephesians 1:3)

75) I am chosen in Christ to be holy and blameless before God. (Ephesians 1:4)

76) I am predestined and determined by God as His adopted child. (Ephesians 1:5)

77) I am sealed with the Promised Holy Spirit. (Ephesians 1:13-14)

78) I am made alive with Christ. (Ephesians 2:5)

79) I am raised up and seated with Christ in heaven. (Ephesians 2:6)

80) I am God's workmanship made new in Christ to do the work of ministry. (Ephesians 2:10)

81) I have direct access to God through the Spirit. (Ephesians 2:18)

82) I am seated in heaven, because Christ lives in me. (Philippians 3:20; Ephesians 2:6, 19)

83) I am able to do all things through Christ. (Philippians 4:13)

84) I am delivered from the power of Satan's principalities and transported to Christ's Kingdom. (Colossians 1:13)

85) I am strategically aligned with God to do Christ's work.

DAILY AFFIRMATIONS

As you step into the miracle of this new season, speak life over yourself. Declare these words every day and watch your transformation unfold before your eyes.

Read chapter 6: Pray..Wait...Hear in "The Way Out" companion book.

86) I demonstrate Christ's love for the unlovable & unloved.

87) I am positioned to do the impossible because Christ lives in me.

88) I give without expecting anything in return.

89) I take this day, by the reins and shake evil out of it because I have dominion over it, in the Name of Jesus.

90) I am diligent and unshakeable.

91) I move with precision and accuracy because the Holy Spirit lives in me.

92) I am bold and tenacious.

93) The forces of evil will not overtake or overshadow me in this day.

94) I am strong in the lord and in the power of his might. (Ephesians 6:10-17)

95) I am strong and courageous because Christ lives in me. (Deuteronomy 31:6)

96) I demonstrate my faith by giving generously and acting justly with others. (Psalm 112:5)

97) I cast out fear and I move with assurance that God is with me. (Isaiah 41:13; 2 Timothy 1:7)

98) I am the lender, not the borrower and I am the head, not the tail. (Deuteronomy 28:12-13)

99) I am blessed to be a blessing. (Genesis 12:2)

100) Father God, prove Yourself Strong & Mighty in me today. Amen.

SCRIPTURES FOR SPIRITUAL WARFARE

Don't recite these scriptures. Pray them. Decree them and they will be established in your life. Be bold as you pray and decree them and watch God move.

1) "In all these things, we are more than conquerors through Him who loved us." Rom. 8:37

2) "Not by might nor by power, but by My Spirit,' says the Lord of hosts." Zech. 4:6

3) "Behold, I have given you authority to tread on serpents and scorpions, and over all the power of the enemy, and nothing shall hurt you." Luke 10:19

4) "The thief comes only to steal and kill and destroy. I came that they may have life and have it abundantly." John 10:10

5) "The Lord will cause your enemies who rise against you to be defeated before you. They shall come out against you one way and flee before you seven ways." Deut. 28:7

6) "And you will know the truth, and the truth will set you free." John 8:32

7) "Do not be overcome with evil, but overcome evil with good." Rom. 12:21

8) "The reason the Son of God was made manifest was to destroy the devil's work." 1 John 3:8b

9) "One of your men puts to flight a thousand, for the Lord your God is He who fights for you, just as He promised you." Josh. 23:10

10) "Do not fear them, for the Lord your God is the one fighting for you." Deut. 3:22

11) Only by your power can we push back our enemies; only in your name can we trample our foes. Psalm 44:5

12) For by thee I have run through a troop; and by my God have I leaped over a wall. Psalm 18:29

13) It is God that girdeth me with strength, and maketh my way perfect. Psalm 18:32

14) He maketh my feet like hinds' feet, and setteth me upon my high places. Psalm 18:33

15) He teacheth my hands to war, so that a bow of steel is broken by mine arms. Psalm 18:34

16) Thou hast also given me the shield of thy salvation: and thy right hand hath holden me up, and thy gentleness hath made me great. Psalm 18:35

17) You have armed me with strength for the battle; you have subdued my enemies under my feet. Psalm 18:39

18) "Truly I tell you, whatever you bind on earth will be bound in heaven, and whatever you loose on earth will be loosed in heaven. Again, truly I tell you that if two of you on earth agree about anything they ask for, it will be done for them by my Father in heaven." Matt. 18:18-19

REFLECTIONS

Use this space to write down what you are hearing from the Holy Spirit as we complete this section. Everything you're experiencing is important to the process of transformation.

R
E
F
L
E
C
T

THE WHEEL
of life

The wheel of life is a great tool that helps you better understand what you can do to make your life more balanced. Think about the 8 life categories below, and rate them from 1 - 10. Answer honestly.

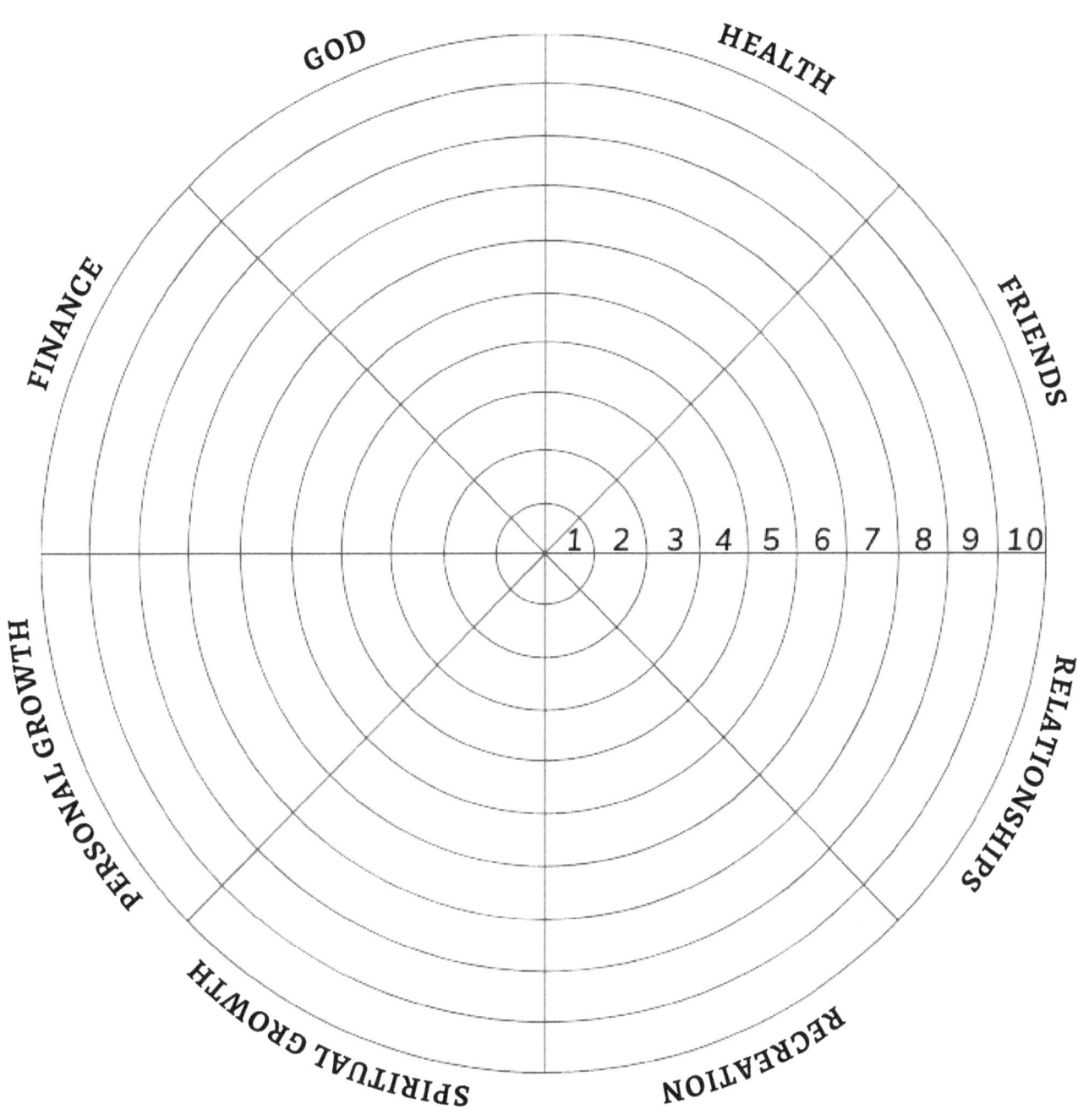

SELF AWARENESS
assessment

Read the promts below and think about the first thing that comes to mind. Fill your answers out in the blank boxes.

I AM A HUMAN BEING THAT...

LOVES	
WANTS TO	
IS DRIVEN BY	
IS INSPIRED BY	
HAS A HABIT OF	
IS HAPPIEST WHEN	
BELIEVES IN	
WOULD GIVE	
WILL ONE DAY	
HAS THE GOAL OF	
WHO NOTICES	
IS AFRAID OF	

LIFE
goals

For each of the categories below, write down things you are doing well and where you need improvement. Take the time to reflect on these, and write a goal for each category.

CATEGORY	WHAT I'M DOING WELL	WHERE I NEED IMPROVEMENT	MY GOALS
GOD			
FAMILY			
FRIENDS			
WORK/ SCHOOL			
HEALTH			
SPIRITUALITY			

BRAINSTORMING
activity

Action brainstorming can help identify what things are
helping or stopping you from achieving your goals.

MY GOAL:

STOP
DOING

DO
LESS OF

KEEP
DOING

DO
MORE OF

START
DOING

SMART GOALS
settings

When setting goals, make sure it follows the SMART structure referenced on the previous page. Use the questions below to create your goals.

S Specific

What do I want to accomplish?

M Measurable

How will I know when it is accomplished?

A Achievable

How can the goal be accomplished?

R Relevant

Does this seem worthwhile?

T Time bound

When can I accomplish this goal?

Goal Setting

GOALS

ACTIONS TO TAKE

MOTIVATIONS

STEPS

POTENTIAL PROBLEMS

PROGRESS TRACKER

GOALS SETTING

For each of the categories below, write down things you are doing well and where you need improvement. Take the time to reflect on these, and write a goal for each category.

	SPIRITUAL DEVELOPMENT	RELATIONSHIPS	PERSONAL DEVELOPMENT	RESOURCES
3 Month				
6 Month				
9 Month				
1 Year				

MY NOT
to do list

List all of your biggest distractions under the "Everything on my plate" list, and then categorize them in the boxes on the right.

EVERYTHING ON MY PLATE

OTHER PEOPLE'S RESPONSIBILITIES

STUFF THAT'S OUT OF MY CONTROL

STUFF THAT DRAINS ME

STUFF THAT DOESN'T NEED TO GET DONE

TRANSFORMATIONAL PRACTICE
exercise

Emotional
Mind

Spirit
led
Mind

Reasonable
Mind

Emotional Mind

Can you think of a time when your emotions felt really strong and took over your thoughts and actions? What were those emotions, and how did they impact your decision-making?

_____

_____

_____

_____

_____

Spirit-led Mind

Can you describe a situation where you were able to use both your emotional and Spirit-led thinking to make a decision? How did you access your Spirit-led mind in that moment, and what was the outcome of your decision?

_____

_____

_____

_____

Reasonable Mind

Think of a time when you relied heavily on logical thinking and reasoning to make a decision. Did you consider your emotions at all in that situation? What about the Spirit-led portion of your mind? How did you balance the need for rational thought with the importance of emotional or Spirit-led awareness?

_____

_____

_____

_____

LEAVING YOUR
comfort zone

What makes you afraid of leaving your comfort zone?

How can you overcome the fear of leaving your comfort zone?

What will happen if you only stay in your comfort zone?

What will your life look like after you leave your comfort zone?

ACTION PRIORITY
matrix

Making the Most of Every Opportunity

Score tasks based on their impact and the effort needed to complete them. (the scale is 0-10 with 0 being for no real effort or impact and 10 being for a major effort or impact).

Activity	Impact (0-10)	Effort (0-10)

priority
matrix

After completing the action priority worksheet, use your scores to plot these activities in one of four quadrants. Prioritize appropriately, and delegate or eliminate low-impact activities.

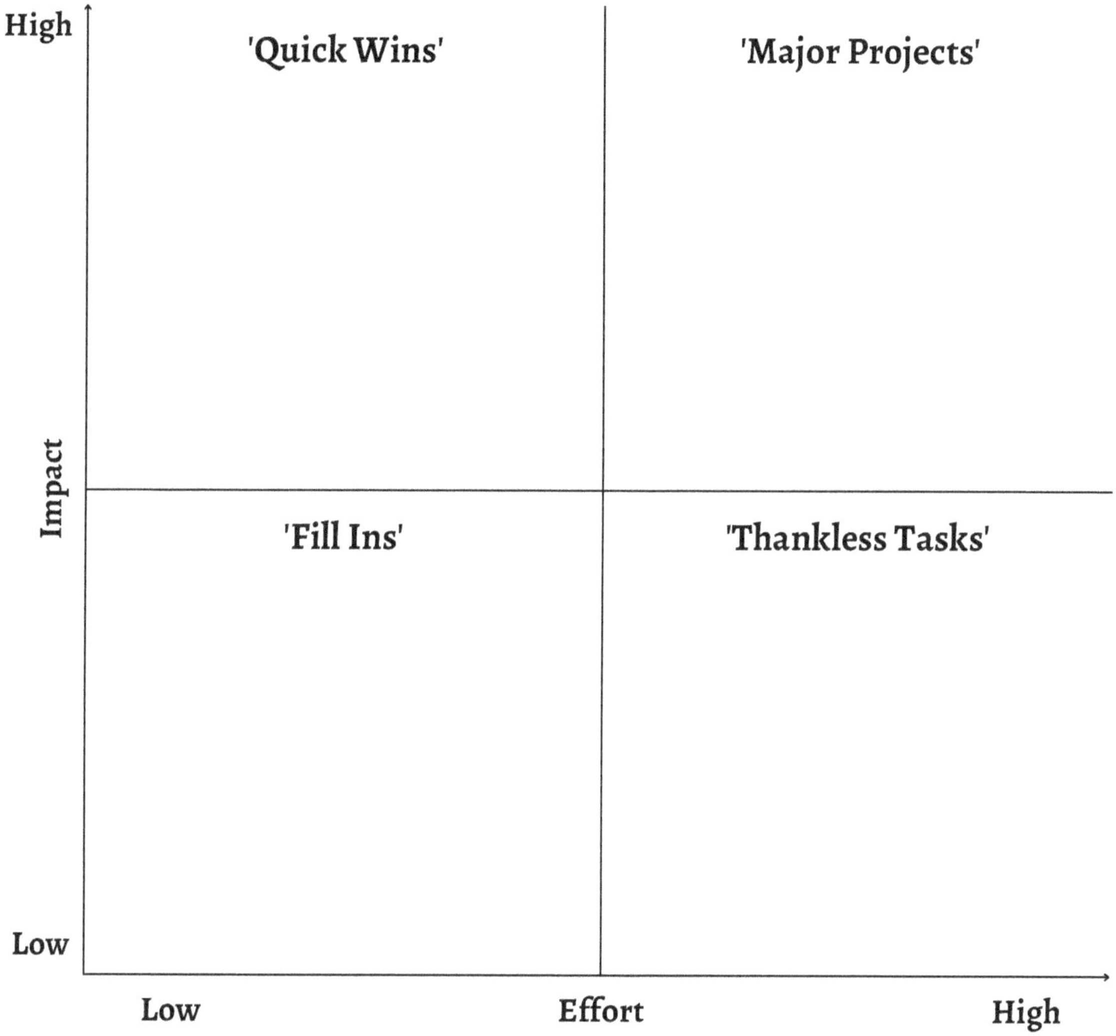

High — 'Quick Wins' / 'Major Projects'

Impact

'Fill Ins' / 'Thankless Tasks'

Low

Low — Effort — High

IMPORTANT NOTES

TAKE STOCK AND
take action

NOTE: Don't overthink your answers. Write down whatever comes to mind.

1. **Tolerances**   (What are you putting up with at the moment?)

2. **Shoulds**   (What do you think you should be doing right now?)

3. **Frustrations**   (What things are frustrating you?)

4. **Desires**   (What do you really want right now?)

5. **Feelings**   (How do you currently feel and want to feel?)

Review your answers above, then imagine and write down what you will do to address each lesson learned within the next few week:

1st Key Observation _____

Action 1 _____

2nd Key Observation _____

Action 2 _____

THOUGHT
awareness

Think about how you handle stressful situations. Don't suppress any thoughts. Let them run their course while you observe them, and write down your thoughts as they occur.

Negative Thoughts

The next step is to rationally challenge the negative thoughts. Look at every thought you wrote down and ask yourself whether the thought is reasonable. How do you release the negativity?

Spirit-led Thoughts

Use Spirit-led, positive thoughts and affirmations to counter negative thinking. See if there are any opportunities that are offered by it.

Positive Thoughts

THOUGHT
transformation

Changing Your Response to Negative or Stressful Situations

Thought transformation is useful for understanding what lies behind negative moods. These may undermine our performance, or damage our relationships with other people.

Step 1: Identify the Situation

Describe the situation that triggered your negative mood.

Step 2: Analyze Your Mood

Describe how you felt in the situation, and how you're feeling now.

Step 3: Identify Automatic Thoughts

Make a list of your automatic thoughts in response to the situation.

Step 4: Find Objective Evidence

Write down any evidence you can find that supports the automatic thoughts and any evidence that contradicts the thought.

Step 5: Monitor Your Present Mood

Take a moment to assess your mood. Do you feel better about the situation? Is there any action you need to take? Write down your present mood, along with any further steps that you need to take.

DAILY CHART FOR
prayerfulness

Meditation

Awareness

Compassion

Prayerfulness Chart

Pray
Scripture

Wait / Hear
the Spirit

Prayer is a two-way form of communication. There's a time to speak and a time to listen. Then there's the waiting...and while we wait, we work.

_____

_____

_____

_____

_____

PRAYERFULNESS
worksheet

Consider what you should pray for as you reflect on what and who needs your intercession.

Consider what you should pray for throughout the week as you focus on what and who needs your intercession.

Consider what you should pray for throughout the month as you reflect on what and who needs your intercession.

PRAYER JOURNALING
weekly planner

A clear vision, led by the Holy Spirit's direction, gives you a tremendous feeling of confidence and personal power. Use this space to capture thoughts inspired by your time with the Holy Spirit. Make copies of this page as you need to. You will eventually need a notebook, not a journal page because God has so much that He wants to deposit in you.

PRAYER JOURNALING
weekly planner

A clear vision, led by the Holy Spirit's direction, gives you a tremendous feeling of confidence and personal power. Use this space to capture thoughts inspired by your time with the Holy Spirit. Make copies of this page as you need to. You will eventually need a notebook, not a journal page because God has so much that He wants to deposit in you.

PRAYER JOURNALING
weekly planner

A clear vision, led by the Holy Spirit's direction, gives you a tremendous feeling of confidence and personal power. Use this space to capture thoughts inspired by your time with the Holy Spirit. Make copies of this page as you need to. You will eventually need a notebook, not a journal page because God has so much that He wants to deposit in you.

Daily
checklist

Wake up early and start your day with prayer and meditation

Make your bed and tidy up your living space

Exercise or stretch for at least 30 minutes to get your blood flowing

Have a nutritious breakfast to fuel your day

Write down your top priorities and schedule your tasks for the day

Take breaks throughout the day to pray so that you avoid burnout

End your day with a prayer of thanksgiving to God for a successful day

WEEKLY Check-in
checklist

	M	T	W	T	F	S	S
Pray and meditate for 10 min							
Deep breathing							
Walk for at least 15 min							
Talk to friends							
Journal for 15 min							
Read the Bible							
Exercise or run for 30 min							
Healthy diet							
Take vitamins							
No technology 30 min before bedtime							
7-8 hours of sleep							

NOTES

_____

_____

_____

_____

SPIRITUAL HABIT
tacker

Keeping track of your spiritual habits can help you stay on track and achieve your goals. Fill out your top 12 goals and mark them off each day you successfully complete them.

WEEK OF: _____

SPIRITUAL HABIT STEP

	S	M	T	W	T	F	S
01	○	○	○	○	○	○	○
02	○	○	○	○	○	○	○
03	○	○	○	○	○	○	○
04	○	○	○	○	○	○	○
05	○	○	○	○	○	○	○
06	○	○	○	○	○	○	○
07	○	○	○	○	○	○	○
08	○	○	○	○	○	○	○
09	○	○	○	○	○	○	○
10	○	○	○	○	○	○	○
11	○	○	○	○	○	○	○
12	○	○	○	○	○	○	○

REFLECTION NOTES

_____

_____

_____

Transformation
excercise

"Let this mind be in you that was also in Christ Jesus..." Phil 2:5. It is important to have a 'focused' mindset in order to realize your goals. You need to be able to face and overcome challenges and barriers with a positive attitude. Assess yourself by answering the questions below:

HOW WILL YOU REMAIN FOCUSED ON HEARING FROM HOLY SPIRIT?

WHAT WILL YOU DO WHEN NEGATIVE THOUGHTS ENTER YOUR MIND?

HOW WILL YOU HANDLE CHALLENGES TO REACHING YOUR GOAL?

HOW WILL YOU REMAIN CONFIDENT WITH A CAN-DO ATTITUDE?

HOW WILL YOU STAY MOTIVATED TO REALIZE YOUR GOAL?

PROGRESSION
worksheet

You were overlooked for that promotion that you and everyone else knew you deserved but they hired someone new who is less qualified than you. How do you respond? Can you forgive them for this? Will you remain in your position?

_____

_____

_____

The same aunt that talked about how fat you were as a child and that you would never amount to anything is now sick and wants to see you. Did you ever forgive her for treating you so poorly? Will you go to see her in the hospital? Can you let bygones be bygones?

_____

_____

_____

Your friend betrayed you by hooking up with your boyfriend after he broke up with you. She was your confidante when things went wrong with him but now she's planning to marry him. Can you forgive her? How do you let go of that pain?

_____

_____

_____

You've been on two dates with a coworker but now he has forced himself on you and raped you. Unfortunately, you still have to see him at work. Now, you've found out that you're pregnant. How will you deal with this? Can you forgive him? Will you have the baby or will you abort it?

_____

_____

_____

6 WAYS TO REACH
Balance

Ignore your phone
for a while

Try to reduce your
perfectionism

Exercise, pray, and
meditate for
relaxation

6 Ways To
Reach Better
Work-Life
Balance

Don't be in a rush to
reach your life goals

Set your priority on
prayer

Reset your life structure:
God, family, others

We all deal with distractions on a daily basis. It's important to learn how to reset and establish boundaries. Setting priorities helps you obtain balance in your life. This exercise suggests a set of priorities to use as you cultivate your own plan.

_____

_____

_____

Overcoming

Once you've formulated your plan and begin to implement it, spiritual battles will come. You will learn how to exercise authority as you go through the process. This is where the Holy Spirit helps you develop personal, and divinely orchestrated strategies for overcoming every situation.

Guard your freedom so that you stay free and out of the weeds.

BE ON YOUR GUARD

"Be on your guard; stand firm in the faith; be courageous; be strong. Do everything in love." 1 Corinthians 16:13-14 NIV

OPPOSITION

Dealing with opposition to your transformation will be part of the process. Read John 8, where Jesus enters the Temple and confronts the establishment that insists on keeping things going their way. This system that is against you will appear to be people but the source is Satan. They may appear as:

- Family

- Friends

- Foes / Enemies

- Note: This is where you reshape your sphere of influence. Who do you bring close and who do you put distance between you? Stand in your newfound Truth with boldness, but don't become brash. This is about setting boundaries.

ASSOCIATIONS

Watch your associations and guard your freedom against those that want to entrap you. Don't allow access to those that want you to slide down their slippery slope, trapping you back into slavery to sin again.

GUARD YOUR GATES

- Guard your eye gates.
- Guard your ear gates.
- Guard your mouth gate.
- Guard your nose gate.
- Guard what you touch (hands).
- Guard your mind (thoughts).
- Guard your Faith (beliefs).
- Guard your Feet (where you go).

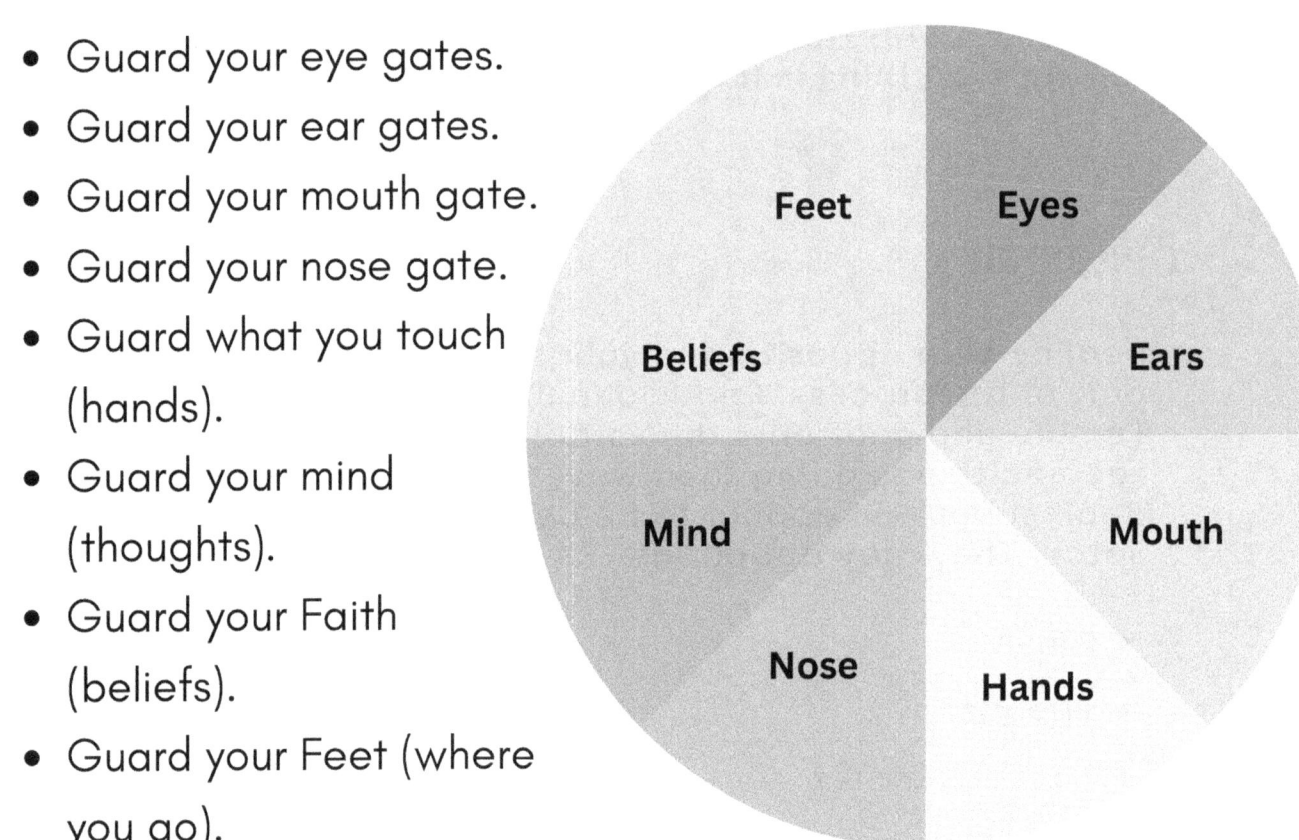

Proverbs 4: 23-27 NLT "Guard your heart above all else, for it determines the course of your life. Avoid all perverse talk; stay away from corrupt speech. Look straight ahead, and fix your eyes on what lies before you. Mark out a straight path for your feet; stay on the safe path. Don't get sidetracked; keep your feet from following evil."

idol WORSHIP

How are idols used by Satan?

Exodus 20:2-6

"I am the Lord your God, who brought you out of the land of Egypt, out of the house of bondage. You shall have no other gods before Me. You shall not make for yourself a carved image—any likeness of anything that is in heaven above, or that is in the earth beneath, or that is in the water under the earth; you shall not bow down to them nor serve them. For I, the Lord your God, am a jealous God, visiting the iniquity of the fathers upon the children to the third and fourth generations of those who hate Me, but showing mercy to thousands, to those who love Me and keep My commandments.

No
Graven
Image

"YOU WILL HAVE NO OTHER GODS BEFORE ME."

Do Not Exalt Anything or Anyone Above God, Including Symbols As Your Savior or Healer (2 Corinthians 10:5-6)

Prayer

Dear Father God, I ask You to renew my mind with Your word in Romans 12:2. In the name of Jesus, I demolish and cast down every negative thought, pretension, false argument, accusation, and lofty thing that would exalt itself against the knowledge of our Lord and Savior, Jesus. Through the power of His Blood, I take captive every one of my thoughts and make them obedient to Christ (2 Corinthians 10:4-5). I surrender all anxious or fearful thoughts to you, Lord Jesus. Through my prayers, I make my requests known to you, knowing that you will answer and guard my mind forever filling me with your peace. (Philippians 4:6) Thank you Jesus for changing my thoughts to be more like you for my thoughts now dwell on what is true, noble, right, pure, lovely and of a good report (Philippians 4:8). I praise you for the power and authority that you've given me to tread upon serpents and all the power of the enemy (Luke 10:19). Because I serve you, you are my shield and buckler (Psalm 91:4); I fear nothing but You. Enlarge my capacity to love like you so that I am that city on a hill that cannot be hidden anymore. Move within me so that we change the world. I decree Your Kingdom has come, Your will be done on earth as it is in Heaven (Matthew 6:10). For the kingdoms of this world are now the kingdoms of our Lord and of our Christ (Revelations 11:15)! I seal this prayer in the Blood of Jesus, for no repercussions, no backlashes, and no revenge from Satan and his forces. I said so; therefore, it is so, in Jesus Name. Amen.

DEALING WITH
Opposition

NOTE: Guard your freedom so that you aren't taken back into slavery to sin.

1. **Family**

   What are you putting up with at the moment? Don't let their labels redefine who you are now. Does their view align with the new you?

2. **Friends**

   What do you think you should be doing right now? This is where you reshape your sphere of influence. Who's important to your future you?

3. **Enemies**

   What things are frustrating you? All enemies aren't bad. Some of them help to push you to reevaluate the direction that you are going.

4. **Work**

   What do you really want right now? Prioritize relationships that enhance you, not just for career goals but also personal and spiritual goals.

5. **Church/ Organization**

   How do you currently feel and want to feel? Are you growing in this place? Do they see where God is taking you? Stand firm in your newfound identity.

Review your answers above, then imagine and write down what you will do to address each learning within the coming weeks/months:

1st Key Observation _____

Action 1 _____

2nd Key Observation _____

Action 2 _____

Things to Remember

01   Reevaluate & test your plan.

02   Do the work.

03   Shortcuts don't exist here.

04   Savor your progress when it happens.

05   Forget about what or who broke you.

06   Reward & register the breakthroughs.

07   Don't waste the failures. They create opportunities.

08   Miracles manifest when God becomes the center of your existence.

09   We're all becoming something.

10   The next chapter of your life may look scary and a little tough. Just keep going.

Notes

Date: _____

Notes

Date: _____

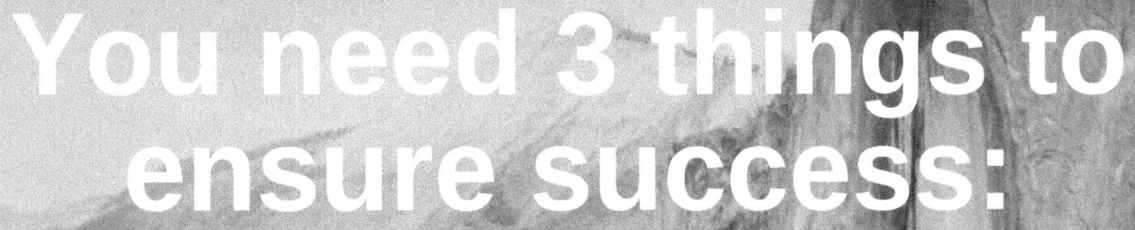

You need 3 things to ensure success:

- A willingness to change

- A road map

- A clear destination

THANK YOU

FOR BEING PART OF MIRACLE MOVEMENT

We appreciate your participation in this Master Class. Your investment in your future will produce a harvest and that harvest will be exactly what God originally intended for you. I'm excited about where God is going to take you next. Please keep us informed about your progress and if there are more educational resources that you would like for Miracle Movement to provide.

Lauraine White

BOOKS WRITTEN BY LAURAINE WHITE

Chosen

Originally published in 2016, Lauraine White pushes the bar while telling much of her life's story. She tells of how God opened a door for her to witness, first hand, the inner workings of international ministries in order for her to see the new age of idol worship. It was and always will be an abomination to God.

The Way Out

After some very traumatic events in her life, Lauraine White, needed a way out. This story, inspired by those events, is told along with how she got out. The message is simple and clear. Jesus is our only way out.

Bulletproof

Inspired by a dream, Lauraine White delivers a call to action message to the Church to come back to its first love and do the work that it is called to do, especially in times like these when many have fallen away from the Truth.

MASTER CLASSES OFFERED

THE WAY OUT MASTER CLASS

Prepare to embark on a journey of discovery. You are here by divine design and being called to God's Army. This call requires that you be equipped with not just any weapons but by those that make demons quiver.

In this workbook, Lauraine shares exercises that will push you to prepare a workable life plan. The work you will do will launch you into your destiny. You will laugh, cry, and realize that you are meant for so much more than what you thought. God's original plans for your life begins now.

BULLETPROOF MASTER CLASS

A prolific writer and speaker, Lauraine White comes with a bold project-Bulletproof Master Class to educate and equip believers in Jesus Christ. These lessons enlighten students on how to overcome the battles brought on by our adversary, Satan. Through bible study and practical exercises, Lauraine leads her students to understand the keys of the Kingdom of Heaven that gives us authority over all the powers of Satan. When this is understood, dominion on earth can be realized. These processes are tried and true methods she used, under the direction of the Holy Spirits to find her own way out of some very dark places. Prepare to be challenged and motivated to see Jesus in a whole new way. He's worth a second look.

LEAVE US A
REVIEW

We hope you enjoyed our Master Class and found lots of value to help you! We would appreciate if you wouldn't mind taking the time to leave us a review.
Thanks!

Lauraine White

THANK YOU FOR YOUR FEEDBACK!

JOIN THE MOVEMENT!

AND BECOME A PART OF THE TRIBE TODAY!

We're building a community of believers that stand on the word of God that says we are a chosen generation that will perform the greater works that Jesus said that we would. If you agree with this mission, please consider joining our community as we connect our faith for the impossible to become possible. We look forward to seeing you at other courses, either on Zoom or live and in person at our retreats and other events. Stay tuned.

MIRACLE MOVEMENT

COPYRIGHT NOTICE

www.miracle-movement.com

Limits of Liability and Disclaimer of Warranty
The author and publisher shall not be liable for your misuse of this material. This book is strictly for informational and educational purposes.
Warning – Disclaimer
The purpose of this book is to educate and entertain. The author and/or publisher do not guarantee that anyone following these techniques, suggestions, tips, ideas, or strategies will become successful. The author and/or publisher shall have neither liability nor responsibility to anyone with respect to any loss or damage caused, or alleged to be caused, directly or indirectly by the information contained in this book.

Cover Design by: Veezie Forbes Design Studio, Atlanta, GA
Photography by: Neiko James of Chris Perfect Studios & Gerren K. Clark

THE WAY OUT MASTERCLASS

BY LAURAINE WHITE
MIRACLE-MOVEMENT.COM

GET IN TOUCH

 INFO@MIRACLE-MOVEMENT.COM

 + 1 770.912.3894

 @MIRACLEMOVEMENT

 MIRACLEMOVEMENT